THE ART AND SCIENCE OF
POWERFUL BUSINESS WRITING

M U SHAH

Chennai • Bangalore

CLEVER FOX PUBLISHING
Chennai, India

Published by CLEVER FOX PUBLISHING 2024
Copyright © M U SHAH 2024

All Rights Reserved.
ISBN: 978-93-56486-19-5

This book has been published with all reasonable efforts taken to make the material error-free after the consent of the author. No part of this book shall be used, reproduced in any manner whatsoever without written permission from the author, except in the case of brief quotations embodied in critical articles and reviews.

The Author of this book is solely responsible and liable for its content including but not limited to the views, representations, descriptions, statements, information, opinions and references ["Content"]. The Content of this book shall not constitute or be construed or deemed to reflect the opinion or expression of the Publisher or Editor. Neither the Publisher nor Editor endorse or approve the Content of this book or guarantee the reliability, accuracy or completeness of the Content published herein and do not make any representations or warranties of any kind, express or implied, including but not limited to the implied warranties of merchantability, fitness for a particular purpose. The Publisher and Editor shall not be liable whatsoever for any errors, omissions, whether such errors or omissions result from negligence, accident, or any other cause or claims for loss or damages of any kind, including without limitation, indirect or consequential loss or damage arising out of use, inability to use, or about the reliability, accuracy or sufficiency of the information contained in this book.

Thank You, Esteemed Readers!

"I am sure the techniques, strategies, ideas, and practical tips covered by this excellent presentation can make anyone's writing fascinating, attention-catching, reader-connecting, and result-oriented."

— Parag Patil, Sr. Consultant, New Delhi

"No book on this subject has offered such practical tips on business writing. If implemented, these tips can substantially improve the quality of business writing."

— Rahul Chaturvedi, Business Head, Mumbai

"Good presentation, Shah Saheb."

— Raghu Prasad Pidikiti, DCS Ltd., Hyderabad

"Thanks for sharing a valuable document, Sir."

— Swamberjit Singh, AGM, Bygging India Ltd., New Delhi

"Excellent tips for powerful business writing–the writing that can change the belief of the reader and make him buy your message."

— Chintan Shah, Proprietor, Handy Logistics, Mumbai

"This is, indeed, a handy guide. The author has emphatically conveyed the critical importance of a result-oriented approach in business writing with a laser-like focus."

— Rohit Mehta, Proprietor, Mumbai

"Wonderful business writing strategies, techniques, and tips packed with pearls of priceless wisdom. The book gives ample examples to drive home the point. A must-read for all business executives."

— Kinjal Shah, Director, Kipraa Enterprise, Mumbai

"I always thought my English was very good, though my first language is French. My myth got busted when I started needing an English-French dictionary to read Mr. M. U. Shah's business letters. In my professional career, I found most business executives' letters easy to reply to, but not so with his letters. His letters are so well-conceived that he doesn't leave any weak links that you can pick up and develop your reply from thereon. Business differences apart, I learned a lot about the art of business writing from Mr. Shah's correspondence."

— Veron, Project Director, Paris

"I have been searching for a manual on this topic for a long time. I even downloaded a couple of paid presentations from Google Play, but none met my requirements. Your detailed and well-structured document has met my requirements. Excellent document, indeed!"

— Sham Sunder Sharma, Gammon India Ltd. Mumbai

"The book highlights the importance of enriching relationships in business so profusely that readers get instantly motivated to start focusing on relationships. The author has coined the beautiful concept of 'Opening an emotional account with the customer'. For the first time, I realised that enriching relationships with customers is as important as good business writing. The tips provided in the book are practical, actionable, and immensely valuable."

— Ankit Prabhu, Head SBU, Bengaluru

FOREWORD

I am delighted and privileged to write this Foreword for Mr. M. U. Shah's latest book, **'The Art and Science of Powerful Business Writing'.**

In the construction industry, my association with the author spans over a long period of time. The topic of artful business writing has been close to the author's heart. The author has always been an excellent communicator with the top management, particularly for vision and goal setting and seeking and firming up managerial decisions. He is equally at ease when communicating with team members with focused clarity about shared task accomplishments. The strategies, tools, techniques, and tips prescribed in the book have been put into practice by him and have worked with remarkable success.

Customer relationship management is an important area that involves extensive communication, including updates on products and services from the viewpoint of time lines for delivery and ensuring all quality aspects. Accordingly, the topic of how to foster enriching relationships with customers is extensively discussed in the book. The author has coined the unique approach of opening an emotional account with the customer for sustainable relationships.

Foreword

Packed with deep insights and priceless wisdom, the book is a must-read for all corporate executives. I am sure this book will provide easy reading pleasure and assimilation tips for day-to-day business writing.

Happy reading!

    Sd/-

V. Suresh, FIE, FRICS, FACCE, HoF-IGBC
Former Chairman and Managing Director, Housing and
Urban Development Corporation (HUDCO)
Chairman, IGBC Policy and Advocacy
Chairman, National Building Code of India
Former National President, NAREDCO
Former President, Indian Buildings Congress

CONTENTS

Foreword v
Contents vii
Preamble viii
Preface ix
The Layered Learning Technique x

1. What This Book Can Do For You 1
2. The Art Of Powerful Business Writing 2
3. The Science Behind Powerful Business Writing 17
4. The Writing Process: Conceiving, Drafting, Revising, Editing, And Vetting 24
5. Practical Tips For Business Writing 40
6. Business Writing: Laudable Strategies And Avoidable Syndromes 61
7. How To Foster Enriching Business Relationships 86
8. The Real-Life Examples Of Business Writing 102
9. Contractual Claims In The Construction Industry 130
10. Conclusion 141
11. Appendices 142
12. Bibliography 202

About The Author 203

PREAMBLE

Do you hesitate to write business letters? Do you freeze at the thought of writing to senior executives? Do you fumble for the right words or tone in your documents? Do your reports raise more questions than answers? Do your e-mails to your colleagues or business associates remain unanswered? Do your proposals fail to win customers? Do you find that your boss ignores even meritorious suggestions or recommendations offered by you? Do you wonder why some writers accumulate hundreds of thousands, even millions, of views on their content, whereas others write and write, only to go unnoticed?

If these questions arise in your mind, you are not in a minority. These are the most common questions that arise in everyone's mind, especially junior business executives. There are many books available on this subject, but there is no single book that answers all of those questions. This book was conceived to provide answers to such common questions that arise in everyone's mind.

The initial version of the book was in the form of a PowerPoint presentation delivered to fellow corporate executives who were looking for a comprehensive solution to their business writing needs. This PowerPoint presentation underwent uncountable rounds of painstaking refinement after each workshop. The phenomenal success of these workshops and their popularity inspired the author to compose this wonderful treatise.

PREFACE

Many of us think writing is not a big deal. We often remain complacent, thinking that ideas matter, not the writing. However, writing is as important as ideas, if not more. While good writing can bring even poor ideas into the limelight, poor writing can result in even good ideas going unnoticed. Based on the merit of ideas and the quality of your writing, they form an opinion about you, your team, your organisation, and its level of professionalism. Therefore, we need to treat business writing as a serious business and adopt a professional approach to our writing.

As you grow in the hierarchy of your organisation, your writing skills, as well as other soft skills, take precedence over your technical knowledge or domain expertise. While poor writing fails to win people over, mastering the art of business writing can set you apart. It can propel your career to its pinnacle. That is why what leaves your desk should be an artful masterpiece.

This book is for those who continually seek to improve their business writing skills and aspire to reach a level of exemplary excellence with every writing endeavour. The author has developed his own personal toolkit of writing strategies, headline structures, techniques, tools, and proven styles; all of which have been painstakingly refined over the years. The book will make you capable of creating a vibrant masterpiece that your reader will love to read and act upon.

Happy reading!

THE LAYERED LEARNING TECHNIQUE

Consider using the Layered Learning Technique suggested below to derive the maximum benefit from this book:

Layer 1: The first time you read the book, you only get an overview. A few specifics may stand out, but by and large, the book's message will fade quite fast unless you layer it on some more.

Layer 2: The book's central idea is now clear to you and will not fade quickly. At this stage, highlight the points that appeal to you.

Layer 3: Upon the third reading, you understand the book well, and the details stand out. You are now able to recite the insights from the narration. The impressions created in your subconscious mind are now available when needed. This is the time to pause and listen to your heart and mind. You can now relate the materials to your life and see their practical applications. Your mind now slowly begins to function at an active 'how-to-apply' level. Prepare a written, time-bound Action Plan for ideas or tips you feel are worth implementing.

Refresh your memory by conducting periodic reviews of the highlighted portion of the book and quantitatively evaluating the progress achieved on the personal Action Plan you prepared.

Update yourself periodically with the latest materials on the subject.

Multiply the knowledge gained by sharing it with others.

1

WHAT THIS BOOK CAN DO FOR YOU

*T*his book is for you if you want to achieve exemplary excellence in your business writing. The book provides valuable strategies, techniques, tools, and ideas. Packed with hundreds of powerful and actionable tips, the book will make your writing fascinatingly artful and result-oriented.

Using this book as a guide, you can improve your ability to do the following:

- Overcoming hesitation in business writing and pushing yourself past writer's block
- Crystalising and organising your ideas
- Selecting the right strategy and timing
- Expressing your main points clearly with a laser-like focus
- Selecting the right words and phrases
- Striking the right tone
- Trimming the fat from your writing
- Creating reader-oriented writings
- Grabbing and holding readers' attention
- Making writing impactful with belief-changing power
- Making the reader buy your message and motivating him to act
- Engineering business response from the reader as per your plan
- Developing transformational relationships with your customers

2

THE ART OF POWERFUL BUSINESS WRITING

2.1 COMMON MYTHS ABOUT BUSINESS WRITING

Do you subscribe to one or more of the following common myths that prevent you from attempting business writing?

- Writing is not my forte.
- My English is not good.
- I don't have a command of the English language.
- I have a limited vocabulary.
- My knowledge of grammar is poor.
- What if mistakes happen?
- Will my customer get annoyed?
- What will my boss say?
- Will I get into trouble?

Good writing is not necessarily an inborn gift. Writing clearly and persuasively is neither magic nor a secret. It's a learnable skill. Like any other skill, anyone can learn this skill, learn it quickly, and overcome writer's block.

Good writing takes careful, conscious work and relentless practice. It doesn't require a flash of genius. You don't have to be Shakespeare or Shashi Tharoor.

2.2 GENERAL WRITING vs. BUSINESS WRITING

There is a notable difference between general writing (such as academic or fiction writing) and business writing. Business writing is a purposeful piece of writing that conveys relevant information to the reader in a clear, concise, and effective manner and aims to obtain a successful business response from the reader. It focuses on expressing opinions in the form of recommendations supported by factual data and information. On the other hand, the purpose of academic writing is different, though it also focuses on facts. Academic writing aims to impart knowledge. Similarly, in fiction writing, the author puts his imaginary ideas or thoughts into engaging words.

2.3 OVERALL BUSINESS COMMUNICATION SYSTEM

No business can work in isolation. All business entities need to continuously communicate with the external world using various means of communication. The purpose of such writing may vary from business to business. For instance, in the medical field, doctors are required to write research reports and articles for journals. Similarly, salespersons need to develop a persuasive pitch for a potential deal, while equipment manufacturers have to write concise and user-friendly manuals for their equipment. Lawyers are required to write their statements of claims or defences.

Business entities need to communicate with customers, vendors, banks, stakeholders, and government departments. For this purpose, business entities use various means of communication, like letters, offers, quotations, contracts, reports, instruction manuals, newsletters, bulletins, articles, advertisements, etc. While each of the above means of communication has its specific place in the business communication system, business letters form an important part of it. Business letters are meant to exchange information in written form while conducting business. The business letter, with its timeless format and principles, remains a powerful means of written communication.

Proficiency in letter writing is a critical aspect of effective communication. Letter writing is the best barometer of writing skills in general. If you can write good letters, you can write just about anything. This is because letter writing helps you focus on others. When writing letters, you connect with a particular recipient with a unique, tailor-made strategy. Letters help you build goodwill with people. Letter-writing skills are the safest way to practice and prepare yourself for more challenging writing tasks. You can't establish yourself as a professional author unless you first master letter-writing skills. Hence, start your journey as a writer by writing letters. Use letter writing as a stepping stone to more challenging writing. Develop the habit of writing letters. Write a few letters every week. Practice writing different types of letters, like thank-you letters, congratulatory letters, letters of recommendation, complaint letters, letters to the editor, and personal notes. Write personal notes to congratulate office colleagues or business associates on promotions. Write personal notes to tell your staff how much you appreciate their hard work. Write to motivate team members to meet goals. Let the new business associates know you are excited to start collaborating and look forward to meeting them personally.

While writing a letter, pay attention to all aspects of good writing. To write a good letter, keep it neat and simple. Place your ideas plainly in simple words and as briefly as possible. Use short sentences that are easy to comprehend. While it's easy to write long, rambling sentences, concise, clear writing requires quality time. Blaise Pascal once said, "I apologise for the length of this letter. I did not have time to make it shorter." Take extra pain and condense your letter to one page. Make it warm and friendly. Use more of you than I. Use tasteful, mature stationery. A letter should be regarded not merely as a medium for the communication of intelligence but also as a work of art. The way the beauty of words, tone, and manner adds a charm to speech, so the selection of words, striking the right tone, organising the text, general appearance of the letter, and elegance of stationery enhance the pleasure bestowed by a letter. While an official business-related e-mail message may make an impression, a handwritten personal letter leaves a lasting impression. Handwritten notes catch attention. If you receive a stack of mail, the handwritten one comes to your attention first. They're personal and, if well done, memorable and saveable. They will help you build and maintain relationships.

Apart from communication with the external world, business entities also communicate internally within the organisation with its employees. Though the purpose of internal communication differs from that of external communication, the underlying principles are the same.

The principles, strategies, techniques, and tools described in the book are based on the context of the construction or infrastructure industry. Many of the examples cited in the book belong to the construction industry. However, these principles, strategies, techniques, and tools apply equally to all other industries. Similarly, while the book predominantly focuses on developing business letter-writing skills, the strategies, techniques, and tools provided in the book apply equally to other types of business writing.

2.4 THE IMPORTANCE OF BUSINESS WRITING

Never underestimate the importance of good business writing. People with a casual approach have gotten their organisations into serious trouble and lost their jobs writing ill-conceived letters. A poorly phrased or poorly reasoned letter may lead to bad decision-making. An ill-structured report can obscure important information and cause readers to overlook vital facts. Readers are likely to set aside and forget a heavy, uninviting proposal. An ambiguous letter or e-mail may require corrective communication to clear up a misunderstanding. It costs us time and goodwill. Similarly, a poorly drafted pitch to an important customer may consume higher-ups' time to repair the damage. If your writing is artless and sloppy, they may assume your thinking is also the same. If your writing is poor, they may even decide you're not worth doing business with. The stakes are that high. Hence, treat business writing as a serious business.

2.5 BROAD CATEGORISATION OF BUSINESS WRITING

Business writing broadly falls into the following four categories:

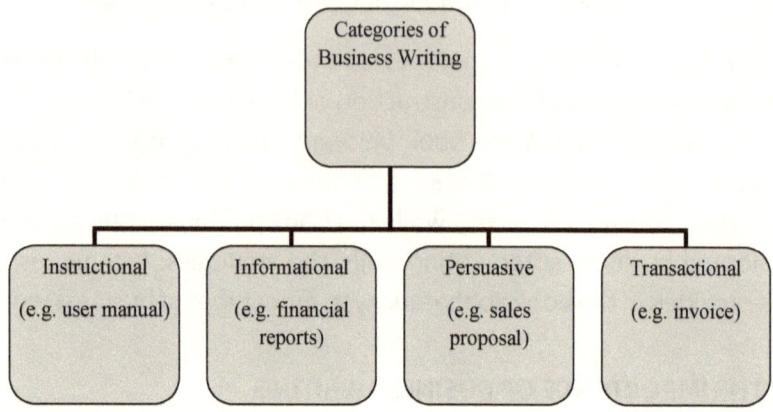

2.5.1 Instructional

Instructional business writing is directional and aims to guide the reader through the steps of completing a task. A user manual falls aptly into the instructional category. Internal documents like Standard Operating Procedures (SOPs) are also part of such instructional business writing.

2.5.2 Informational

Informational business writing pertains to recording and reporting business information accurately and consistently. It comprises documents essential to the core functions of the business, for outlining plans, tracking growth, and complying with legal obligations. The financial statements of a company, presentations to investors, capital investment plans, etc. are examples of informational writing.

2.5.3 Persuasive

The goal of persuasive writing is to impress the reader and influence their decision. It conveys relevant information to convince them that a specific product, service, company, or relationship offers the best value. This type of writing is generally associated with marketing and sales. It includes proposals, bulk sales emails, press releases, etc.

2.5.4 Transactional

Communication related to day-to-day transactions falls into this category. The bulk of such communication may be through email but also includes official letters, standard forms, invoices, etc.

2.6 SPECIFIC OBJECTIVES OF BUSINESS WRITING

Within the above broad categories, each business communication has a specific purpose that is intended to be accomplished. The purpose may include informing, enquiring, exploring new opportunities, ordering, selling, entering into a contract, approving, reminding, appreciating, complaining, claiming compensation, defending demands for compensation, etc. Depending on the purpose to be achieved and the target audience you want to reach, you need to select the most appropriate communication instrument.

If you choose a letter as your communication instrument, first determine your goals for the letter. Objectives for any given letter should be as few as possible. If there are too many things to be accomplished, consider writing a separate letter for each objective. If the situation demands including more than a couple of objectives for a given letter, decide the priority, focus accordingly, and work out an appropriate strategy. Before you start drafting the letter, your strategy should be crystal clear in your mind.

Besides immediate objectives, each letter should also promote long-term objectives like building sustainable and rewarding relationships, enhancing the organisation's image or brand value, and, more importantly, not jeopardising any such long-term objectives. For example, should you write a hostile letter to your customer if you are frustrated by an overdue, outstanding payment? While such a hostile letter may or may not get your payment released, it will surely damage your long-term relationship with the customer. Should you shoot out such a hostile letter when the damage it can cause is certain, but the benefits are uncertain?

2.7 ESSENTIAL CHARACTERISTICS OF A GOOD WRITER

A good business writer should have a deep understanding of human psychology in general and the likes and dislikes of the addressee in particular. In addition, a good writer must pay attention to many other aspects, which include:

- An intense focus on the reason for writing
- A thorough understanding of the reader's needs
- A strong, passionate belief in what you are writing
- An ability to express an idea precisely
- An ability to express an idea in a logical sequence for seamless flow
- An ability to strike the right tone appropriate to the objective of the letter
- An appreciation for the right words for the right places
- A preference for words as simple as possible
- An aversion to business jargon and business speak
- A feel for natural idiom
- Sound knowledge of grammar
- A good sense of humour

Believe that you can write. Anyone can become a professional writer with practice. Relentless practice can make your writing perfect. You also need to develop the habit of reading extensively. Read well-written material every day. Read newspapers and journals. Study the writings of professional writers. Daily, read at least one piece aloud with an appreciation of the phrasing, the pacing of ideas, the punctuation, the paragraphing, etc. Read with feeling. Start paying attention to the style of The Wall Street Journal, its word choice, sentence structure, and flow. Writing for business has evolved in recent times. Grammar and style also evolve. The standards keep changing. For example, almost all style guides now state that judicious use of emoticons is acceptable in business writing. That is why business writers need to continually hone their writing skills to stay current with conventions by reading online resources about business writing or taking a business writing course. Invest in a guide to style and grammar for reference. Garner recommends Fowler's Modern English Usage.

2.8 ESSENTIAL ATTRIBUTES OF GOOD BUSINESS WRITING

Though in all types of writing substance matters, in business writing it matters the most. The most critical element in business writing is the information it conveys. At its core, business writing is about information exchange, and hence the information contained in your document is the foundation of good business writing. The information must be truthful, accurate, complete, and relevant to the reader. If any of the above attributes are missing, the document will fail.

Besides, writing well also requires a lot of planning, strategising, tactfulness, and diplomacy. Apart from the merit of your idea, how you present it is also equally important. You can have all the great ideas in the world, but if you can't communicate effectively, nobody will hear them. Remember, sentiment lives not only in what is being communicated but also in how it is being communicated. Good writing is about capturing and communicating ideas, painting pictures, persuading prospects, motivating readers, and changing their beliefs. This needs to be done with an ample dose of vibrancy, liveliness, and resilience. Your entire personality is smartly deployed to create a vibrant masterpiece that the reader would love to read and act upon. Don't approach it in a dull or uninteresting way that leaves the reader bored or unmoved. It is about achieving your objectives with personality and vibrancy. It is not just about selecting appropriate words or using error-free language; it goes much further. It encompasses many aspects, from how to address the recipient and sign your name to the conventions of business vs. social vs. personal letters to the most elegant way to fold the sheet. It is not only about the craft of writing letters, but also about the conceptual elements of composition and the role of letters as social currency. Osmosis is all the more important today, when cold screens and electronic text have left the written word homogenised and devoid of expressive form. Above all, many times we need to avoid direct messages, especially if they are unpleasant or negative. Unpleasant or negative messages need to be conveyed with extra care. You may have to sugar coat such negative messages.

While good writing is easy to understand, economical, and straightforward, poor writing is confusing, long-winded, and unconvincing. Good writers communicate their ideas to the world effectively without wasting the reader's time. Poor writers cloud the reader's mind. While poor writers create barriers between themselves and their readers, good writers connect with them. Good writers know their readers and their psychology thoroughly. They know their priorities and goals. They know what pressures they are subjected to and what motivates them. Good writers provoke the thoughts of their readers, transform their beliefs, and lead them to act. Their writing is capable of convincing the readers and motivating them to act. Good writing gets ideas noticed. It gets them realised. If, for example, someone is writing an article or a book on the topic of 'Belief in God', his article or book should be so powerful that it should convert atheists (non-believers in God) into theists (believers in God). Such conversion is the best measure of the book's success, rather than the number of copies sold or reviews of the books.

Also, well-written business correspondence creates a good impression. Whatever your profession, you need to develop good business writing skills. It consists of presenting accurate, well-written information that prevents misinterpretation. It is a test of your communication skills. Good writing reflects your level of professionalism and credibility. Sharp, precise writing skills enable you to clearly articulate presentations and important topics succinctly or concisely. A tailored piece of writing can help an employee rise above the crowd.

Overworked managers with little time might think that improving their writing is a tedious or even frivolous exercise. However, remember, even your business audiences are busy—very busy. They will ignore you if you don't get to your point quickly. Don't make them struggle to understand your message. If you make them struggle, they may stop reading your message. Hence, knowing how to fashion an interesting and intelligent sentence is essential to communicating effectively, winning business, and setting yourself apart.

A good business writing needs to have many attributes; important among them are:

• Clear	• Concise and brief
• Specific	• Credible
• Well-structured	• Ease of scanning
• Accurate and precise	• Neatly readable
• Creative and imaginative	• Complete in all respects
• Full of liveliness	• Passionate
• Implicit	• Relevant
• Coherent	• Objective
• Reader-oriented	• Consistent
• Persuading	• Respectful and well-mannered
• Positive and optimistic	• Result-oriented
• Friendly-toned	• Appropriate
• Neutral and impartial	• Non-hostile
• Error-free	• Tactful
• Sincere	• Truthful and ethical
• Culture sensitive	• Timely
• Powerful	• Motivating
• Unbiased	• Non-discriminatory

2.9 THE ART OF POWERFUL BUSINESS WRITING

A large vocabulary does not necessarily create powerful writing. Even with a limited vocabulary, some prominent writers, like Barack Obama, write so powerfully that people who utterly disagree with him also find it deeply moving. Powerful writing requires many attributes. We need to pay attention to each of these attributes if we want to master the art of business writing.

2.9.1 Powerful writing is reader-oriented.

We need to be reader-oriented if we want our writing to be powerful. Writing that is self- or writer-oriented can never be powerful. Powerful writing focuses on the reader's needs, intent, and purpose. Powerful writers don't write what they want to say; they write what the reader wants to read or cares about the most. Powerful writers adopt a reader-oriented approach. The reader-oriented approach means presenting things from the readers' perspective and making them feel that we value them dearly and that they are really important to us. It means stepping into the reader's shoes and looking at things from their perspective. It entails wearing the reader's hat. It entails wearing the reader's glasses. It means using magnifying glasses and microscopically examining each sentence in each paragraph from the reader's perspective. A good writer knows his reader intimately. He knows his pulse. He knows the language he understands, the beliefs he shares, and the knowledge he holds. He is aware of the assumptions he can and cannot make about the reader. He articulates the content and tone, keeping in mind the addressee and his temperament. Good writing isn't boring because the writer knows what will hold his reader's interest. It is neither too dense nor too simple for the intended reader; it's just right. It uses more of you and yours instead of I, me, my, mine, we, us, or ours. It avoids beginning the letter with 'I' or 'We'. Good writing exploits the power of 'YOU'. Where possible, address the recipient directly. Addressing the reader directly in a formal letter makes the content engaging, making the recipient feel that you are talking directly to him. Using third-person addresses as 'one' can excessively formalise the content, which is out of place in most contexts. For instance, it would be more appropriate to say, "You need to develop a personal rapport with your customer," rather than, "One needs to develop a personal rapport with one's customer."

2.9.2 Powerful writing is passionate.

Good writing is about passion. It is something important that the reader already cares about, or something the writer makes them care about through his writing. And you can't make the reader care unless you care, with a deep sense of sincere belief, about whatever you're writing. You need to be strongly passionate about what you are writing. If you lack a strong passion, your writing cannot make your reader do what you expect him to do. A half-hearted approach rarely brings results. For example, suppose you are writing an article about the benefits of using Artificial Intelligence (AI) in business. Can your article make any worthwhile impact if you are not convinced about the benefits of using AI in business yourself? To make your article impactful, you need to genuinely believe in the benefits of using AI in business and be passionate about the same.

2.9.3 Powerful writing is focused.

The purpose of good writing is to achieve a specific goal. That goal might be to sell something, to convince someone of something, to change someone's belief, or to seek some favour. Each sentence in each paragraph must lead the reader towards the goal. It is best to remove anything that doesn't guide the reader towards that goal.

2.9.4 Powerful writing uses the right tone.

The tone in writing refers to the writer's attitude toward the reader and the subject of the message. The overall tone of a written message affects the reader, just as one's tone of voice affects the listener in everyday interactions. Using a respectful and formal style that matches your purpose, audience, and context ensures your message comes across the right way. The tone should be appropriate for the topic, purpose, and audience, reflecting well on the writer and connecting with the reader. Your writing becomes reader-oriented when you select an appropriate tone that aligns with the purpose of communication. For example, if you are writing a newsletter for your customers, use friendly and plain language to target your goals. If you are writing a business proposal, use a professional and persuasive writing tone. If you aim to make your writing conversational, it's fine to end a sentence with a preposition now and then, especially to improve flow and avoid awkward construction.

As general guidance, the business writer should strive for an overall tone that is confident, courteous, and sincere; that suitably mixes emphasis and subordination; that contains non-discriminatory language; that stresses the 'you' attitude; and that is written at an appropriate level of difficulty. Use polite and positive language. Avoid using negative or harsh words that may offend or antagonise your readers. Avoid slang, colloquialisms, indecent humour, sarcasm, discriminatory language, or emoji that may be inappropriate or misunderstood. Business writers should communicate in a non-discriminatory language that expresses equality and respect for all individuals. A non-discriminatory language treats all people equally. It does not use any discriminatory words, remarks, or ideas. Discriminatory language can create a barrier between you and your reader. Hence, make sure your writing is free of bias. Don't discriminate based on race, ethnicity, religion, age, sexual orientation, or disability.

The level of difficulty should match the competence of the reader. For example, if you are submitting a Structural Audit Report for a residential building to the members of a housing society (who are not engineers), you can't use high-sounding technical terms that only a qualified civil engineer can understand. You need to avoid such technical terms and concepts. You need to present your findings in a language that a layman can understand. On the other hand, if you are submitting a Structural Audit Report on a distressed bridge to the Chief Engineer, PWD, you can't use simple language. Here, you have to explain your findings using Civil Engineer's language. Similarly, you must explain a biopsy report to a patient in a language that the average person can comprehend.

That said, while many businesses have their own style guides and basic rules for style and grammar, you must follow these rules in your writing to maintain a professional image. Sloppy writing, poor word choice, or an unearned, overly familiar attitude can come back to haunt you.

2.9.5 Powerful writing is concrete.

Abstractness tends to result in writing that is particularly limp and empty. When the subject on which you are writing is real and non-abstract, it may be relatively easy to convince your reader. However, convincing your reader, even when the subject is an abstraction, is the real challenge to your writing skills. In such situations, good writers ground their topic in the real world through examples, metaphors, analogies, and storytelling. This is an intensification of the old 'Show, don't tell' rule. Powerful writing doesn't just tell; it shows, through examples and analogies, how, in the real world, this has already been accomplished or can be accomplished. For example, if you are submitting a tender for a flyover, don't merely make a general statement that your designs are economical, but give quantified details as to how much savings you achieved for your customer in your recent flyover project.

2.9.6 Powerful writing flows seamlessly.

Good writing is all about making the various elements that make it fit together neatly and draw the reader along. Flow means that everything in a piece of writing is exactly where it should belong. For example, whatever you need to understand paragraph no. 3 is present in the preceding paragraphs, i.e. paragraph no. 1 or paragraph no. 2. Each part transits seamlessly into the next, and the style and tone remain consistent throughout the letter. Easy-flowing writing should be coherent and move seamlessly and effortlessly from one part of the letter to another.

2.9.7 Powerful writing develops gracefully.

Powerful writing is not just focused on a goal; it leads the reader inescapably towards it. That may be through the use of evidence in support of an argument, through the relaying of a narrative describing events occurring chronologically, or in some other way, but it must be graceful—without gaps of reasoning, unsupported assumptions, missing information, or anything else that would cause a reader to stumble.

2.9.8 Powerful writing is fearless.

Fear is not a helpful emotion in organisations: it constrains ideas and wears people down. Quite rightly, then, good organisations will try hard to minimise fear in the workplace. We can ascertain the level of fear in any organisation by having a look at the language people use. People often resort to impersonal, jargon-laden writing due to fear of reprimands, fear of standing out, fear of taking responsibility, and fear of sounding stupid. The more confident people are, the more independent they feel, and the higher the probability that their writing is creative. Fearless writers express what and how they think. They don't follow the herd.

2.9.9 Powerful writing is compelling.

Powerful writing demands attention, whether through the importance of its topic, the force of its cogent argument, or the strength of its language. The writer makes it so compelling that the reader doesn't want to stop reading, even when he is done.

One of the most appropriate examples of powerful writing is one project where we had to collect a huge refund of Works Contract Tax deducted at source from our bills. The case went up to the Appellate Tribunal. We hired a senior chartered accountant-cum-lawyer who prepared a sixteen-page prayer. The Chairman of the Tribunal said, "I read through your sixteen-page prayer in one sitting. When I reached the last page and the last paragraph of the prayer, I couldn't prevent myself from picking up my pen and writing, "Agreed. Accepted." What can be a better yardstick for powerful writing than one that motivates the reader to act as desired by the writer?

2.10 THE FOUR GATEKEEPERS

All of us want our communication to be interesting and engaging for our readers and want them to act. How do we ensure this? Here is the simple test. Our communication, before it is sent out, must pass the following four Gatekeepers:

1) Gatekeeper No. 1

Is it saying something of interest to the reader? If not, stop here and rethink it, or rewrite it and make it reader-oriented.

2) Gatekeeper No. 2

Is the writing full of empathy towards the reader? Show some real understanding of issues, concerns, or the environment people are in.

3) Gatekeeper No. 3

Is it truthful? Untruthful writing may give you some benefits in the short run, but it can never benefit you in the long run.

4) Gatekeeper No. 4

Could you read it aloud in public without feeling embarrassed? If you feel embarrassed while reading it aloud in public, surely it needs rewriting.

3

THE SCIENCE BEHIND POWERFUL BUSINESS WRITING

3.1 SCIENCE OF FEEL-GOOD CHEMICALS

Many people, especially in the corporate world, believe that good writing is only an art, and that those who write well have an innate talent they've further honed through experience, intuition, and practice. This is only partially true. Business writing isn't just an art; it's also a science. Every day, we're learning more about the science of good writing. Advances in psychology and neurobiology show, with data and through images, how exactly the brain responds to words, phrases, and stories. Brain scans can clearly reveal what entices readers. From unexpected plot twists to colourful metaphors, it appears there is a scientific strategy for creating content that delights readers on a primal level and releases those feel-good chemicals. This means that the criteria for making better writing choices are more objective than we might think. It is possible to scientifically design our personal winning formula that consistently crafts good writing—writing that is reader-oriented and makes a desired positive impact.

Contrary to the perception of business writing as a purely clinical and efficient means of communication, it possesses the potential to emotionally uplift and stimulate readers, akin to the impact of great works of literature. Nike's famous 'Just Do It!' slogan, for example, has influenced the temperament of countless youths. Just a single great line of business writing shaped multiple generations.

Human beings like to be appreciated. They love to be appreciated. This urge has been present since time immemorial. This urge is independent of geography, gender, or any other aspect. Whether people are from European countries or Asian countries, they all like to be appreciated. Whether male or female, they all like to be appreciated. In fact, girls value appreciation more than boys, particularly when it pertains to their beauty!

The science behind the phenomenal success of social media has its roots going back to the fundamentals and basic urges of human beings. If someone posts something on social media and receives many likes, he is motivated to create another post, and this way, he continually strives to maximise his likes. The addiction to receiving these likes is so strong that he spends countless hours preparing his posts at the expense of his other activities. This is because likes generate dopamine spikes in the human body. Dopamine is a chemical messenger (neurotransmitter) that works in the brain. It helps nerve cells send messages to each other. It's produced by cells deep in the brain and acts on cells in other parts of the brain. Dopamine is known as the 'feel-good' hormone. It gives you a sense of pleasure. It also gives you the motivation to do something when you're feeling pleasure. When you praise someone, his body releases the dopamine hormone, and the whole alchemy of the body changes for the better. Appreciation conveyed verbally, in person, or in writing through written communication generates dopamine spikes. This is understandable. However, even virtual appreciation, such as a thumbs-up emoji, can be equally effective in triggering dopamine spikes. Social media creators have capitalised on this basic human urge and exploited it fully for their commercial objectives.

The above strategy's applicability extends beyond social media. This strategy can be applied universally to any business and also to various aspects of life. We get pleasure when we drink refreshingly hot coffee, eat delicious food, take a soothing bath, or receive an enveloping hug. Similarly, well-executed prose makes us feel pleased, which makes us want to keep reading. Good writing gets the reader's dopamine flowing in the area of the brain known as the reward circuit. Good writing causes spikes in dopamine release. Great writing releases opioids that turn on reward hot spots. Good writers know this, and accordingly, they generate dopamine spikes through their writing. Recent research has revealed the reasons why such dopamine-hike-oriented writing is effective.

Kent Berridge, a pioneering psychologist and neuroscientist from the University of Michigan, explains:

> *"Researchers originally believed that the reward circuit largely handled sensory cues. But, it has now become clear, based on neuroimaging studies of the last fifty years, that all kinds of social and cultural rewards can also activate this system.*
>
> *Whether it's a succinct declarative statement in an email or a complex argument in a report, your writing has the potential to light up the neural circuitry of your readers' brains. The same is true if you read the words to an audience. The magic happens when prose has one or more of these characteristics: it's simple, specific, surprising, stirring, seductive, smart, social, or story-driven. In my work as an author and writing coach for businesspeople, I've found those eight S's to be hallmarks of the best writing. The scientific evidence supports their power."*

A skilled business writer must also grasp the nuances of the relationship dynamics between themselves and their readers. The writing differs depending on the relationship. Are you aiming to write content that appeals to loyal and familiar customers, or are you targeting prospective ones? The former permits a more familiar and friendly writing tone, while the latter demands a focus on establishing credibility. Possessing these skills enables you to define your purpose and audience and provides a clear framework for both what and how you write.

3.2 HOW TO EXPLOIT THE POWER OF SCIENCE IN BUSINESS WRITING

Several techniques exist for harnessing the power of science in business writing. A few such techniques are described below:

3.2.1 Identifying and focusing on DSIM of the readers

One of the important lessons taught in public speaking is the lesson of delivering an impactful punch. The punch should score high on the Dominant Self-Interest Motive (DSIM). Good speakers identify the

DSIM of the audience and design their speech around that DSIM. They demonstrate genuine concern for their audience and make their speech audience-oriented. A similar concept also holds good in business writing. Unless you address the DSIM of the reader in your communication, your communication is unlikely to create interest for the reader.

When you identify the Dominant Self-interest Motive of your readers and focus your writing on such a DSIM, it works wonders. Your readers' attitude toward your writing changes. He reads your writing with a bias because he feels that it will benefit him. Scientists using MRI and PET machines can literally see how reward regions clustered in the midbrain light up when people read certain types of writing or hear it spoken aloud. Each word, phrase, or idea acts as a stimulus, causing the brain to instantly answer a stream of questions: Does this promise value? Will I like it? Will this benefit me? Can I learn from it?

3.2.2 Making writing reader-oriented and reader-friendly

When you make your writing reader-oriented and reader-friendly, your readers are interested in your writing. They read through your writing and complete it without taking up another task midway.

3.2.3 Respecting the readers

When you respect the readers, their self-esteem gets a boost. They form a positively biased attitude towards your writing.

3.2.4 Not antagonising the readers

If you antagonise the reader, its effect is the opposite of when you respect the reader. An antagonised reader forms a negative bias towards the writer. Hence, good writers take extra care and ensure their readers are not antagonised.

3.2.5 Writing in hand

Researchers suggest that writing by hand has a wide range of benefits, from stimulating neural activity in the brain that can lead to a meditative state to boosting creativity and our ability to make connections between ideas to stimulating learning and improving our memory.

3.2.6 Making writing easy to read

When you make your writing easy to read, your readers don't have to exert themselves. On the contrary, if they have to exert themselves to read your message, they may leave reading it midway. Hence, you should aim to get the message across with the least effort.

A simple and uncluttered writing style goes a long way toward communicating the message to the reader. As far as possible, avoid using grandiose writing filled with industry-specific buzzwords and acronyms. Otherwise, the reader may be unable to comprehend the document or lose interest in it. Additionally, it's crucial to make your writing easy to skim, especially for materials such as press releases and business proposals. No one wants to struggle through large blocks of text to find pertinent information.

3.2.7 Using short sentences

A simple version with shorter words and sentences, among other things, scored higher on self-efficacy. Readers who are served such simple versions express more confidence in succeeding. Readers infer that simpler patterns yield better predictions, explanations, and decisions. That means you're more persuasive when you reduce overdressed ideas to their naked state. Short sentences, familiar words, and clean syntax ensure that the reader doesn't have to exert too much brainpower to understand your message. By contrast, long sentences or sentences with clauses nested in the middle take longer to read and cause more comprehension mistakes.

3.2.8 Removing fat

Another tactic is to drill down to what's salient and scrape tangential details. Let's say you have researched five new business opportunities for a construction company and are finally recommending two options in a memo to senior leaders. Instead of exhaustively covering every pro and con of each business opportunity, it may be advisable to pitch just the top two opportunities and identify their principal pluses and minuses.

3.2.9 Using an active voice

The use of an active voice makes sentences easy to understand. In an active voice, the subject of the sentence performs the action. While in passive voice, the subject of the sentence receives the action. For example, 'The Chairman approved the project.' is an active voice. 'The project was approved by the Chairman.' is a passive voice. Similarly, the statement, 'Scientists have conducted experiments to test the hypothesis.' is an active voice. The statement, 'Experiments have been conducted to test the hypothesis.' is a passive voice. Use an active voice to emphasise the person or thing performing an action and a passive voice to emphasise the action that is being performed. Using an active voice makes your business writing clearer, more concise, and more powerful. This is because it avoids ambiguity and confusion. It clearly conveys who's responsible for the action, what the action is, and what the result is. Sentences in active voice are generally, though not always, clearer and more direct than those in passive voice. You can recognise passive-voice expressions because the verb phrase will always include a form of be (i.e. am, is, was, were, are, or been). The presence of a be-verb, however, does not necessarily mean that the sentence is in a passive voice. Another way to recognise passive-voice sentences is that they may include a "by the..." phrase after the verb; the agent performing the action, if named, is the object of the preposition in this phrase. If you write "Recess after a long class is loved by school children," for example, instead of "School children love recess after a long class," you're switching the standard positions of the verb and the direct object. That can reduce comprehension accuracy by 10%, making it take a tenth of a second longer to read.

In most non-scientific writing situations, active voice is preferable to passive for the majority of your sentences. Even in scientific writing, the overuse of passive voice, or the use of passive voice in long and complicated sentences, can cause readers to lose interest or get confused.

3.2.10 Making writing more specific

Specifics awaken a swath of brain circuits. Think of 'peacock' versus 'bird.' Or 'wipe' versus 'clean.' More specific words activate more neurons in the visual and motor-strip parts of the brain than general words do. This implies that the specific words cause the brain to process meaning more robustly. Years ago, scientists thought our brains decoded words as symbols. Now we understand that our neurons actually 'embody' what the words mean. When we hear more specific words, we 'taste,' 'feel,' and 'see' traces of the real thing.

3.2.11 Storytelling

If we want to make our writing interesting, we must use ample stories and analogies. Don't make general statements. If general statements are made, pair them with specific examples. Through story-telling, we can make even abstract topics interesting for the readers. If the stories you present happen to be ones that the readers can relate to themselves, your writing will have a lasting impact. This is because stories have a longer retention period than abstract or dry writing.

4

THE WRITING PROCESS: CONCEIVING, DRAFTING, REVISING, EDITING, AND VETTING

4.1 CONCEIVING

The stage when a need is felt to write something—whether a business letter, a report, or an article is the stage when the writing is conceived. Once such a need has arisen, start conceiving your writing. Don't procrastinate. Don't wait for inspiration to come. Inspiration rarely comes when you want it. Be self-inspired. You need to overcome the initial resistance and the inertia and take the first step in the right earnest with firm determination. Once you take the first step and begin writing diligently, you will no longer require inspiration.

Experienced and professional writers visualise how they want their final product to look, and they keep this in mind when they conceive their writing. However, it may not be advisable for beginners to visualise the finished piece of their artwork at such an early stage. If they do so, worry can overwhelm them. Hence, beginners should first start collecting and organising their raw materials without getting overwhelmed by the tasks ahead. Even during the data collection stage, don't get overwhelmed if the volume of data to be collected is too large; slice the same into smaller tasks.

The more specific and precise your conception, the better will be the quality of your final product. Furthermore, you will accelerate your writing process significantly.

4.2 THE MACJ (MADMAN, ARCHITECT, CARPENTER AND JUDGE) ANALOGY

Any writing project essentially involves a series of tasks. There are many ways in which you can approach your writing. However, all methods essentially involve slicing the writing project into a series of tasks. One such popular method that writers use is the MACJ method. Coined by Betty Sue Flowers, this method involves envisioning such writing as belonging to the following four distinct characters:

- The Madman who gathers materials and generates ideas—whatever comes to his mind.
- The Architect who organises the Madman's raw materials by drawing up a sensible outline.
- The Carpenter who puts your thoughts into words, laying out sentences and paragraphs by following the Architect's plan.
- The Judge, who is your quality control character, refines the entire text, including correcting grammar and punctuation and tightening and polishing the language.

If you carry out these operations in this order, you will be most efficient. Of course, you may always need to retrace your steps, particularly if you're a beginner. While an experienced professional writer may get almost all the ideas in the beginning, a novice may not get all the ideas in the first place. Thus, an experienced writer may not be required to revisit his text substantially. However, the novice will develop more ideas as he writes his text. He may need to draft more material after he identifies the gaps in his writing. Notwithstanding any needs for revision that may arise as you progress, do your best to compartmentalise these discrete tasks and address them in the prescribed order.

Get the Madman started. Business writing requires clarity of thought. Hence, scribble down the main points before you start writing anything for business purposes. You may be writing internally to your boss for approval of your proposal, or you may be writing externally to your customer, pitching for the sale of your product. In either case, it is advisable to scribble down the main points before commencing any writing. If you start full-fledged writing before spelling out the main points, it will be extremely difficult to find a focus for your writing, and you may not be able to convince your reader. Additionally, such writing will require a lot of time to edit and re-edit.

Accept ideas, regardless of their source. The ideas can come from personal experience, memory, observations, research, reasoning, speculation, imagination, or conversations with colleagues. To start with, the ideas can be in random order. As the character suggests, the ideas need to be allowed to be generated irrespective of their merit or, in other words, even if ideas, prima facie, look unsuitable. Hence, at this stage, don't worry about the merit or effectiveness of the ideas. Another character, best suited for that role, will examine the merit or effectiveness of the ideas in subsequent stages. The Madman's job is to generate as many ideas as possible. Many times, the problem you are trying to address may seem intractable, and you may struggle to find a suitable approach. For example, it may be a challenge for you to persuade the folks in the finance department to approve your budget when they are habitually used to turning down such requests left, right, and center. Similarly, persuading your customers to give you more time to submit a report is a challenge. However, don't let these challenges overwhelm you. Avoid obsessing over the magnitude of the challenge. Just collect as many ideas and facts as you can. Generating more ideas goes a long way toward making your first draft nearly perfect. Also, collecting ideas and facts upfront will help you push through your writing task and defuse anxiety about writing.

When you are generating ideas in the capacity of a Madman, it is advisable to keep track of quotations and sources. If you are using someone else's material, put that into quotes or acknowledge the source. Give credit whenever it is due. This is because, if you have borrowed someone else's materials, you may not be able to back them up convincingly. Hence, don't copy other people's materials. This will also avoid accusations of plagiarism against you.

After having done the good groundwork, let the Architect take the lead. When we want to construct our dream bungalow, for example, we hire an Architect. He carefully listens to our requirements and puts our ideas on a proper blueprint, duly deploying his professional skills. A similar role is expected from the Architect here. The Architect organises Madman's raw materials into a sensible outline. He distills ideas into a few main propositions that convey your message. He arranges these raw materials in a logical sequence from the reader's point of view so that even the reader who is not familiar with the topic can understand your message. Arranging these raw materials in a proper order may be a challenge for you. In the past, people would write the text on separate index cards and then arrange these cards in a proper order. Today, with user-friendly word processing technology at our fingertips, it is much easier to rearrange our text, even if we have started writing it in a random order.

You should be primed to write once the Mad-man and the Architect have done their jobs. Schedule the time when the Carpenter is to begin, and when the appointed time comes, get started without procrastination. The carpenter picks up the Architect's blueprint and writes the first draft. You must convert the distinct pieces of text into smooth writing. Smooth writing means a sequence of well-joined sentences and paragraphs, not a mere collection of them. This requires good planning and skill in handling transitions or links that help readers follow the train of your thoughts. Make these connections and transitions as smooth as possible, so that the readers don't notice discontinuities and can move forward seamlessly.

Give the Carpenter a tight schedule. Give priority to the schedule rather than perfecting your text. You may get tempted to perfect your text as you write, but allowing the Judge and the Carpenter to work side by side is counterproductive. This amounts to inefficient multitasking. You are doing two things inefficiently rather than simultaneously. Besides, the brain's editorial part is simply incompatible with the production part. Who needs a fault-finding critic's interference when you are trying to create something creative? You are best at keeping the judge away as you produce your first draft. In any case, you will have to spend plenty of time editing it later.

The role of the Judge involves deliberations, weighing your words, filling or bridging the gaps, amplifying, shortening, sequencing, and so on. Allocate plenty of time for this activity. Do this in several distinct phases, each time focusing only on one element of your writing. Lastly, give the final finishing touch.

If you follow the MACJ process, you will not only automatically get the much-needed inspiration and minimise your procrastinating but also improve the quality of your writing.

4.3 ALTERNATE THREE-STEP METHOD

As an alternative to the MACJ method, you can use a three-step method to draft a letter. This method is almost identical to MACJ and essentially divides the task into the following three steps:

Step No. 1 involves generating a list of topics to cover. This could be in random order. This helps define the universe you want to cover. The topics not included in this list fall outside of your purview. Of course, you may need to add or delete a few topics as you progress further in your writing. However, if such a need arises, you should revise your list and come out with Revision 1 (R1) of your list.

Step No. 2 involves categorising your main points into sets of three and developing these raw ideas into full sentences.

Step No. 3 involves rearranging these points in a logical order, keeping your readers' needs in mind. Since you have defined your horizon and written down three main points, your job has become quite easy.

If you follow this three-step process, your sentences will be shorter than they otherwise would be, your idioms will be more natural, and your draft will start taking shape before you know it. If there is a painful part of writing, it is the first draft. When you shorten the duration, it isn't as painful. Hence, write as quickly as possible. To prevent premature fussing, write against the clock. This is called speed writing. Creative writers often use it as an exercise to get their juices flowing. Allow yourself five to ten minutes to draft each section—the opener, the body, and the closer—and set the timer.

4.4 UNDIVIDED ATTENTION

We all do multitasking. We divide our focus between the phone in our hands and the people at the table. While already in communion with other people or doing other things, we steal a few seconds online. We find it natural to divide our attention between multiple things, all the while being surrounded by noise and distractions. It is rare to find someone who doesn't do this. Though such multi-tasking might appear to be efficient, this way of communicating tempts us to keep real dialogue at bay. It comes in the way of slower and more thoughtful considerations when engaging with one another. In today's world of social media, we offer bite-sized morsels of our thoughts and feelings on our little screens and expect other people to feel adequately addressed, or imagine they will somehow flesh out the rest. But the reality of communication is that, regardless of intention, how we say something can directly affect how others receive it, in ways that affect how they respond to us in kind. Many times, a message sent via instant messaging is lost in transmission, translation, or interpretation and results in a lengthy conversation to undo misunderstandings. Communicating this way does not always save time.

Writing a letter requires you to be still and take the time to gather your thoughts. You cannot write a letter while walking, having dinner, taking a bathroom break from a meeting, or watching television. It requires you to slow down. And when we do slow down, our thoughts have a chance to slow down too and sort themselves out. This way, we get space to note and consider our feelings and time to think about how to choose our words.

Before you put pen to paper or hands on the keyboard, consider what you want to say. "The mistake that many people make is that they start writing prematurely," says Garner. "They work out the thoughts as they're writing, which makes their writing less structured, meandering, and repetitive." Ask yourself: 'What should my audience know or think after reading this email, proposal, or report?' If the answer isn't immediately clear, you're moving too quickly. "Step back and spend more time collecting your thoughts," Blackburn advises. If we jot down points on a piece of paper before we write a letter, it helps to foster clarity of thought before we speak things out into the world. Even if we never post this draft letter, it will crystalise our thoughts and emotions towards the recipient.

4.5 EMPHASIS AND SUBORDINATION

In business writing, many times some points require emphasis while others require subordination. Use appropriate emphasis and subordination techniques, depending on the demands of the script. You can help your readers understand which of your ideas you consider most important by using emphasis. Similarly, subordinating an idea allows you to underplay it.

To emphasise an idea, place it in a short sentence. A short and simple sentence will most effectively convey an important idea. You can provide further explanation, appropriate examples, or evidence in the following sentences. The following example shows how we can convey the emphasis:

"Smoking will no longer be permitted in the building. After studying the data on the dangers of second-hand smoke, the Committee on Employee Health and Safety made an evidence-based decision."

Contrary to this, if you want to subordinate an idea, place it in a compound sentence. You may rewrite the same message as follows:

"We constituted a three-member Committee on Employee Health and Safety with a mandate to examine the effect of second-hand smoke on employee health. The committee met several times, collected a large amount of data, and considered the evidence available in this regard. The Committee unanimously concluded that second-hand smoke is highly injurious to health. Accordingly, they recommended that smoking will no longer be permitted in the building."

4.6 EXPLOIT THE POWER OF CHRONOLOGICAL NARRATION

Business events are inherently chronological; one thing happens and then another. This structure is effective not only in business writing, but also in films and fiction books. The director always presents the films in chronological order, unless a well-conceived strategy dictates a flashback. Barring such specific strategies, films are generally presented in a chronological sequence. This also holds good for fiction novels.

When you take some commercial dispute to your lawyer for presenting your case in court, and if the duration of the project is long, the first thing the lawyer will ask you is to prepare a chronology in a couple of pages. Include the dates of contract signing, the nature of the dispute, and the current status. You may not provide details about every project event, but the lawyer must know at least the major ones. Provide him with a concise timeline of events to help him comprehend the emergence of disputes. Hence, keep your chronology as brief as possible and focus only on the key events that led to the disputes. The lawyer will use these chronological details when he presents the case to the Judge for better appreciation by the Judge.

4.7 EXPLOIT THE GREAT POWER OF GRAPHICS

Present a part of your report in a table, diagram, flowchart, or other visual aid that helps your reader understand the content and its importance. Exploit the power of graphics like diagrams and flow charts to illustrate what is described in the text. Place the graphic close to the text, or on the next page. Use a self-explanatory legend that the reader can easily understand. However, don't overuse graphics or visuals. Graphics or visuals should be used at a minimum—not exceeding 25% of your document, memo, email, report, etc. Too many graphics become confusing and often detract from the message you want to convey. A few powerful, well-placed graphics will accomplish more to get your point across than something that looks like a bad attempt at scrapbooking.

While the use of graphics in reports and PowerPoint presentations has unlimited potential, business letters can only incorporate tables, charts, or graphs.

4.8 EXPLOIT THE STUNNING POWER OF SILENCE

It sometimes seems as though more thoughtful ways of communicating with others are a dying art. The famous 1981 painting "Conversation," by the late Jamaican artist Barrington Watson, is a powerful illustration of this idea.

CONVERSATION

Three Jamaican women dressed in simple skirts and headscarves fill the width and length of the canvas. Rural women on a break from the day's labour, their buckets beside them, they each rest their weight on one leg, hips out, and each is casting their eyes to a point beyond our vision. It's titled "Conversation," but no one's lips seem to be moving. Still, there is a definite mood portrayed. There are surely things to be said, but each woman's posture is determined, almost defiant, as if waiting to see who will make the first move to share what's on her mind. The hands on the hips and the crossed arms could be read as a stubborn refusal to be the first to speak up, to show signs of vulnerability or concern.

This picture reminds us that even the silences we keep or the things we don't say can communicate as much as the things we do. At times, it can be wiser and kinder to remain quiet until we are clear on what we desire our words to convey, in both meaning and effect. A pause from communicating can create the space to determine how we want a relationship to develop further. Words make worlds. And how we use them powerfully shapes the worlds we create between us. Sometimes our silences confuse or fracture relationships, because no one can read minds, and we are left to fill in the blank spaces with our own, often incorrect, narratives. Yet in the art and challenge of communication, so much happens in the space between the words.

4.9 ORGANISING

No matter how smooth your transitions are between sentences and paragraphs, time-pressed readers will zone only if you place a solid wall of text in front of them. Hence, you need to break up your documents with some signposts to lead people from one section to another and help them quickly locate the parts they are particularly interested in. This will also be helpful when they do a second reading of your letter. In the second reading, the reader would like to go through only those parts in which he is interested, and he should be able to find such parts easily. Also, freely use headings, subheadings, numbering, etc. Make your subheadings as consistent as possible. Consistent style and parallel syntax in your writing reinforce the document's logical and rhetorical sequence.

Some writers tend to jump to conclusions in the middle of a building-up argument. They often drive straight into the middle without orienting the readers; the inevitable result is confusion.

4.10 REVISING vs. EDITING

Once you have finished the first draft, you will revise it before you edit it. Have a critical look at your draft and revise it by deleting the unwanted text or adding some additional text and making it complete. Revising is a reconsideration of what you are saying as a whole and why you are saying it. It is a rethinking of the floor plan. It ensures that what you have written makes sense. Editing, on the other hand, is more a matter of fine-tuning sentences and paragraphs.

Following are a few posers that will assist you in performing both of these roles:

ROLE	POSER
REVISER	Is it reader-oriented?
	Is it reflecting empathy toward readers?
	Is it truthful?
	Is it factually correct?
	Have I said all that I need to say?
	Is it complete in all respects?
	Is writing consistent?
	Have I removed all that is not relevant?
	Have I avoided lame repetitions?
	Have I used proper prefixing, when reiterated?
	Have I used creative freshness, when reiterated?
	Is it stated fairly, yet diplomatically?
	Have I avoided a slow wind-up that unnecessarily lingers the message?
EDITOR	What is the best way to phrase the idea?
	How can I make it more interesting?
	Are my expressions relaxed and yet refined?
	Am I gliding from one sentence to another seamlessly, without discontinuities?
	Can I save some words?
	Is my writing unmistakable?
	Is it ambiguous or capable of some other meaning?

4.11 PROOFREADING

Proofread your work. In the good olden days, manuscripts were handwritten or typed, the printing of which required typesetting. The printing presses kept proofreaders on their rolls to compare the typeset text with the manuscript. They used proofreaders to compare texts word-for-word. Proofread your final product in a similar manner. It involves a word-by-word comparison of the final output with the manuscript, if any. If no manuscript was prepared, check whether what was intended to be conveyed has been conveyed. It also involves checking and correcting any grammar, spelling, originality, or style errors. It's a crucial last step to ensuring the quality and professionalism of your business writing. And it ensures you don't damage your credibility or relationship with your reader.

To proofread your work:

- Read your document aloud, or have someone else read it for you.
- Use a checklist or a guide to spot and fix common errors.
- Find and correct common mistakes with a global check using the 'Find and Replace" tool available in MS Word.
- Use word-processing or grammar-checking AI tools.
- Take a break and review your document again with fresh eyes.

4.12 WELL-CONCEIVED SUMMARY

A good summary is focused and specific, and it is usually at the beginning of your documents, though it can be placed at the end in some situations. Don't make your reader dig it. At the outset, get to the point. Don't hold back crucial information.

Make every word count. Shorter is better when it comes to summary. Of course, brevity without substance is worthless. The summary should give a gist of the reasoning in sufficient detail so that there are no counter-questions that require re-explaining. The words used and the length of the summary should be just optimum, neither more nor less. You should draft your summary so well that it cannot be reduced to fewer words, nor does it require additional words to clearly summarise the message.

4.13 FOLLOW UP

"What exactly do you do in the office the whole day, Dad?" asked one innocent young daughter to her father, a CEO of a MNC.

"I follow up, my little princess; I follow up the whole day," replied the father.

If we believe our job ends once we issue a letter, we are mistaken. You are unlikely to achieve the desired results unless you follow up. Therefore, ensure that you follow up personally and persistently until you achieve the desired results. Follow up so much that the other person gets irritated, and to avoid further irritation, he solves your issue. However, don't get this wrong. The word irritation is used only to highlight the frequency of follow-up. As regards the manner of follow-up, you need to deploy your people management skills of the highest order so that follow-up is non-offensive and non-irritating, duly applying a heavy dose of respect to the customer. The follow-up may be required in person and through written communication. You may have to write follow-up letters or reminders. Your follow-up letter is an opportunity to reinforce your strengths, affirm your interest, and, if necessary, respond to any concerns that came up when you personally met them for follow-up. When reminding, use soft and palatable language. Avoid the use of the word reminder. If you use the word reminder, prefix it with 'gentle' or 'humble'.

Apart from the customers and vendors, follow-up is also required internally within the organisation.

4.14 ESCALATION OF ISSUES

> *"We cannot solve our problems with the same thinking we used when we created them."*
>
> **– Albert Einstein**

Suppose the officer to whom you have addressed your letter is unable to act as desired by you even after allowing a reasonable time and despite due follow-up and reminders. In that case, you may have to escalate the matter to a higher officer. Also, refer to para 7.10 in Chapter 7.

4.15 MINUTE INTRICACIES OF MINUTES OF MEETING

Meetings are an integral part of any business. Broadly, there are two categories of meetings. The first category is periodic meetings. Weekly or Monthly Progress Review meetings are examples of periodic meetings. These meetings take place regularly at specified intervals. Many times, meetings are convened for some specific purpose. Meetings convened to solve some technical or other issues, or resolve some differences or disputes are examples of the second category of meetings. These meetings are convened depending on the requirements. Either party can call for the meeting, giving due notice to the other party. It is advisable to circulate an agenda before the formal meeting.

We must record the discussions during the meeting for future reference. The recordings of the meetings are popularly known as Minutes of the Meeting (MOM). It commences with the list of participants who were present during the meeting, followed by a detailed note of the major points discussed, the agreements reached between the parties, and the implementation timelines. MOM should reflect the true and fair picture of what was discussed during the meeting. You can record the points even in the form of bullets.

If you are a contractor, you should volunteer to draft the MOM yourself. This is because the drafter of the MOM has a substantial advantage. The drafter of the MOM can set the tone of the minutes. Also, he has the opportunity to select proper words and phrases that he thinks are suitable from his point of view. Of course, the other party can correct the draft MOM, but even then, the person who has drafted the MOM continues to have an upper hand. The other party, while correcting the draft, will at the most focus on the main points and ascertain whether these main points are recorded fairly from their point of view. They may, in general, not correct the tone, the language, or the words or phrases used to a large extent. To this extent, the drafter of the MOM is in an advantageous position.

Many times, despite the exchange of several drafts, the parties are unable to conclude the MOM. This happens, especially when there are chronic, major differences or disputes between the parties. In such cases, the matter may be escalated to a higher level. Higher-level officers are likely to adopt a balanced approach, and they will be able to arrive at a mutually acceptable draft of the MOM.

It is always advisable to have the minutes signed rather than leave them un-concluded. This is because, in every meeting, there will be at least a few points on which an agreement is reached. If the MOM remains unsigned, even the points on which the agreement was reached are likely to remain unimplemented. Hence, for the aggrieved party, it is always advisable to have the MOM signed. If necessary, it is better to compromise on some issues. This will help in implementing the agreed-upon points.

In the year 2001, a historic meeting took place between India and Pakistan in Agra, popularly known as the Agra Summit. After prolonged discussions between the two Prime Ministers, bureaucrats from both countries sat down to prepare a jointly signed Press Release. However, because of a long-running geopolitical dispute and rigid stands by both countries, they were not able to move forward. The discussions between bureaucrats continued up to midnight, but in vain. The time for Pakistan's Prime Minister to fly back to Islamabad was approaching fast, but there were no signs of both parties arriving at a mutually acceptable draft. Eventually, the Agra Summit was declared an unsuccessful Summit because no jointly signed Press Release could be published. The failure to arrive at a jointly signed Press Release overshadowed the entire discussion during the meeting, which might have taken place in the most cordial atmosphere. This example shows the paramount importance of arriving at mutually acceptable minutes for the meeting.

The G20 Summit, which India hosted in 2023, serves as another classic example. With the involvement of as many as twenty different countries that have strong views on many of the issues, it was not an easy task to arrive at a consensus Resolution, which was acceptable to all the countries. The organisers of the meeting smartly divided issues into two parts. Firstly, they discussed, drafted, and concluded minutes on points that were acceptable to all the countries, leaving aside a few controversial issues. Having done this, it was easy to concentrate further discussions on controversial issues. Lots of discussions took place on these controversial issues. Even a few words or a few sentences were discussed for hours together. However, no agreement was in sight. The deadline for the closing ceremony was approaching fast. Eventually, the big bosses sent a message to the effect that, "You all have two hours to conclude the document; otherwise, the Summit will end without the release of a consensus document."

After this ultimatum, the discussions started again. One group of countries insisted on using phrases like 'war against Ukraine'. This was highly objectionable to another group of countries. Eventually, wisdom prevailed. The above controversial phrase was replaced by the acceptable phrase 'war with Ukraine'. If a top-level directive is given that participants of the meeting will not disperse unless the MOM is signed, many times such directives work.

MOM, being a legal document, necessitates the utmost care in its drafting. Arbitrators place a greater value on MOM than the parties' unilateral correspondence. The planning for the meeting should start with the selection of the right employees as participants in the meeting. It is advisable to select the best employees for the meeting. They should have domain knowledge of the topic of the meeting and, more importantly, persuasive skills to make the other parties agree with your viewpoint. Also, start planning for the meeting from the agenda stage itself. If you want to achieve agreement on some of the points, and reaching an agreement on those points is very crucial for you, it is advisable to exclude controversial points from the agenda stage itself. Such a strategy will help in the finalisation of a mutually acceptable MOM once an agreement on such points is reached. You can then have a separate meeting for controversial points. And even if you are unable to resolve the controversial points in the next meeting, it is fine because you have succeeded in concluding the MOM of the first meeting and got some relief on those issues.

Many times, MOM prepared by one party is sent to the other party by email or post. You may add a note that if no advice to the contrary is received, the understandings stated in the MOM will be regarded as final. Such a practice can relieve the recipient of the need to reply. However, even if such a note is not added to the draft MOM, you can safely treat the MOM as final if no comments are received from the other party despite waiting for a reasonable period.

5

PRACTICAL TIPS FOR BUSINESS WRITING

5.1 GENERAL

- Be selective in replying to correspondence. Remove the myth from your mind that you must respond to every letter. Your strategy should determine whether or not to reply to a particular letter, as well as when and how to do so.
- Letters to all stakeholders are important, but pay particular attention to letters to customers.

5.2 HANDLING PAPERWORK

- Go for a paperless or less-paper office.
- Before you write a paper, consider the cost of your and others' time.
- As a rule of thumb, if you can handle an item in twenty people-minutes or less, do it in person or on the phone.
- Eliminate unnecessary paperwork, such as cover letters.
- Avoid self-protecting or self-congratulating memos, and motivate others to avoid the same.
- Avoid the temptation to look only for good news. Be brave enough to handle unpleasant news.
- Trust people to report exceptions.
- Get reports via audio or videotape.
- Clear at least one terminally troublesome piece of paperwork a day.
- Establish a 'Ritual' whereby you have a Blitz day every month. Get large sacks or boxes and fill them with accumulated junk.

- Think green. Tie up with a local paper recycler to come every week. This will help you and others ruthlessly throw away unimportant paperwork.
- Don't recycle confidential papers; shred them yourself in a shredding machine.
- Conduct zero-based paperwork planning every quarter.

5.3 HANDLING CORRESPONDENCE

- Barring a few vital letters, most of the letters can be replied to when first read. Follow this practice, and you will not be required to read the same letters repeatedly.
- Pull out papers that require top-priority action.
- Decide which item is to be dealt with first in the context of your priorities, not the senders'. Don't follow the urgency label, communication mode, or reminders provided by the sender. Respect the sentiments of the senders of the communication, especially if they are your customers, but not at the cost of delaying your top priority task.
- Make letterhead complete with the full address (not only Post Box No.), pin code, phone, fax, website, email address, and location guidance.
- Use window envelopes to avoid typing the addresses on envelopes.
- Fold your letters properly so they do not need to be turned around to read when unfolded.

5.4 WRITING

- Before writing, ask yourself whether it is absolutely necessary to put it in writing or if a phone call will suffice.
- Develop a reservoir of goodwill. You will get a competitive edge and save time and money.
- Make a checklist of letters you write often.
- Standardise routine letters. For forwarding a document, use standard postcards with fillable blanks.
- While conducting a survey, provide check-off boxes that others can check.
- A quick handwritten note on the original letter can save time. However, don't use red ink. Keep the original and send back the photocopy. Never return the original to the sender.

- Ensure neat penmanship. Write clearly to save minutes down the line.
- Prepare the draft in double space.
- Attach the letter under reply and accompanying papers with the draft.
- Train the secretary to notice the slightest reference to related materials you might need and bring the same along so that the final version is completed faster.
- Correct minor misspellings in pen and avoid reprinting.
- Clearly state the required action and mark it directly to the person concerned.
- Consider pre-empting certain issues if you expect the same to be raised by the customer subsequently, so that back-and-forth correspondence is avoided.
- Don't cover too many demands or requests in a single letter. The reader is more likely to grant only a few demands (which are least harmful to him) and conveniently ignore others.
- Support your contention with the strongest argument first. Also, don't give too many points to support your contention, thinking it will strengthen it. If you give too many points, a few of them are likely to be relatively weak. The reader is likely to pick up the weakest point and reject your contention based on the weakest point, conveniently ignoring other strong points.
- Make your writing brief, crisp, to-the-point, and reader-oriented.
- Believe that many letters need not be longer than a few sentences or, at the most, one paragraph.
- Consider using cryptic telegraphic language. People sparingly use words because the cost of telegrams is based on their word count. Use each word with the cost-consciousness of telegrams.
- Avoid big sentences.
- If lengthy and time-consuming calculations are required, separate them from the body of the letter and go ahead with the letter.
- Use the same phrases as in the contract. If the contract states "Work Completion Report," don't say "Project Completion Report." If the contract states vetting the designs, don't use terms like approving, proof-checking, or reviewing the designs.

- Stay consistent throughout the letter. If in the body of the letter you have referred to Annexure 1, don't label it as ANNEXURE 1, Annexure I or Appendix I.
- Don't use paper to discuss or argue.
- Develop the habit of documenting your success stories, failures, or lessons learned for the benefit of others and publish them suitably.

5.5 THE PURPOSE

- Don't begin writing without precisely knowing what you are trying to accomplish. If the writer himself is unclear about the precise purpose of writing, the reader will also be equally unclear. Readers have no idea where to focus their attention. They are uncertain about how to respond to the message. So plan out what you'll say to make your writing more direct and effective.
- Decide on the desired outcome, which could be approving your proposal, granting you additional time, or awarding you additional work. This purpose should guide what you say and how you say it. Many aspects of writing, such as the selection of words and phrases and the tone of the letter, depend on the purpose of the writing. Hence, it would help if you clearly define the purpose of writing and the outcome you expect.
- Say clearly what you want to convey, and with every sentence, ask yourself whether you are advancing the cause.

5.6 THE DRAFTING PROCESS

- Be determined to start writing. Don't procrastinate.
- Each business transaction has a parent document like the Term Sheet, Memorandum of Understanding, Work Order, Purchase Order, Contract, etc. Don't draft any business letter without reading the parent documents. If required, you can underplay or overplay some provisions of the parent document, which can be a part of your well-conceived strategy, but being aware of the provisions of the parent document is a must. For example, if your contract specifies a time limit of thirty days for approving your drawings, you should be aware of this provision. Remember, such provisions vary from contract to contract. As a

business leader, you may be handling multiple contracts. If a couple of contracts handled by you have such provisions, don't presume that this contract must also have similar provisions. You need to take the trouble of getting up from your chair and picking up the contract document for this project. After ascertaining that such a clause exists in this particular contract, whether you want to utilise this favourable provision in your letter or not is a different matter.

- First, generate a list of points to be covered and decide on the focus and priority.
- While drafting, remember that the addressee is not as immersed in the project as you are. Also, his mind is preoccupied with many other things.
- Remember, you should be writing as if for a specific reader.
- Prepare the first draft as early as possible. Don't procrastinate.
- Convert raw ideas into complete sentences.
- Instead of writing the entire letter from scratch, borrow paragraphs or sentences from your best letters, retained topic-wise, in a folder. However, guard against a tendency to copy and paste blindly.
- Pay due attention to all three parts of the letter: the opening, the body, and the closing.
- The opening should attract the attention of the reader and motivate him to read the whole letter. You don't have to draft the opening at an early stage of the drafting process. Get the bulk of the writing done, and then create the best opening you can. The great authors do this. Provide the required background and links to previous references. Like a handshake or that head-to-toe glance to take in what someone's wearing, your opening creates a first impression that will colour your reader's perception of what you say thereafter. Don't be afraid to use a bit of personality to start building a relationship, and be interested in your reader if you want him to be interested in you. Openings have three functions:
    - grabbing attention. Readers, especially busy ones, are always time-pressed. They have many things to do. Your opening should be interesting, or else they are likely to stop reading and pick up some other task.
    - setting up what comes later. Make a bold statement or raise an intriguing question that a reader will want to see you support or

resolve. However, don't draw a reader in with something compelling or very topical but completely unconnected with what follows. It's misleading and trust-breaking.
  - creating good first impressions. It should establish a lasting first impression.
- The body of the letter is its heart, and it should be capable of convincing the reader so that he starts believing what you believe. You make your case here.
- The letter's closing section should provide a brief summary and the reader's expected action.
- Be precise and specific. Don't make general statements.
- Draft the letter in its entirety. Begin by writing in support of what you are most comfortable addressing. However, if a challenging section stumps you, switch to a more comfortable section and come back. You need to get into the flow. If you are still struggling, when you return to that problem passage, say what you are trying to convey out loud. Sometimes, speaking will help you find the right words. The point is to get your ideas on paper, knowing that you will still have time to elaborate and perfect them at the next stage.
- The main points should not be more than three. The human mind finds it difficult to grasp an excessively large number of points.
- Spoon-feed the reader. If some clause of the contract is crucial for developing the argument, don't merely give reference to the clause number and expect him to open the bulky contract document and search the clause. This is unlikely to happen, and even if it does, it will happen later, when he has free time. Instead, reproduce the clause for ready reference. However, the reproduction must be verbatim without any addition or deletion. If manipulated, reproduction will cost you credibility. You may supply emphasis by colour highlighting, underlining, or using italics or bold fonts, but never make alterations while reproducing. Also, when something is underlined or highlighted, say 'emphasis supplied'; the way judges do in their judgments. Alternatively, attach a photocopy of the relevant clause of the Contract for ready reference and, if required, highlight the portion where you want to supply emphasis.

- Define each term when it first appears. Use a new sentence or paragraph to explain the term a little later, if required. Similarly, define the abbreviation when it first appears.
- Writing is not just a collection of words and figures. It goes beyond being grammatically sound. Also, be a stickler for continuity. Good writing is a cohesive sequence of well-joined sentences and paragraphs, not a mere collection of them. Use well-placed transitional phrases to guide the reader to the next idea, duly establishing the relationship to the previous.
- Don't conclude at the early stage of the letter. Hold it for the subsequent stage of the letter. Meanwhile, if you are specific enough, the reader will draw his own conclusion in his mind. Your skill lies in leading the reader to conclude something close to your conclusion. This strategy is much better than unilaterally expressing your opinion without any supporting logic and hoping that the reader will buy your opinion. The objective of the letter is not merely to express your opinion unilaterally but to make the reader buy your opinion, and if the conclusion drawn by the reader closely matches your conclusion, half the job is done.
- Refrain from preaching or lecturing. Preaching makes the reader feel inferior. Hence, avoid explaining things that are familiar to the reader, and even if the script demands reminding about familiar things, prefix such reminders with phrases like, 'As you are aware, ...'
- Edit, polish, and improve piece by piece, one at a time. Use spellcheck and other software like Grammarly or ProWritingAid to correct grammar, punctuation, etc. Hunt for offending phrases and remove them. Your success may depend on your writing and how it affects readers. That is why what you produce should be as polished as possible.
- Prepare a few more drafts, each iteration improving the letter until the final version is satisfactory.
- Proofread aloud before sending the letter. Read passages out loud. That's where those flaws reveal themselves: the gaps in your arguments, the clunky sentence, and the section that's two paragraphs too long.
- Sharpen your writing skills with relentless practice.

5.7 THE LANGUAGE

- Use plain, simple language. Strive to use simple words and sentences to express an idea accurately. Readers are unlikely to devote their full attention to anything that requires undue effort to understand. Simplicity breeds clarity. If the reader struggles to understand you or has to refer to a dictionary, he will stop trying and think less of you.
- Select the right words; almost the right word will not do. As Mark Twain rightly said, "The difference between the right word and the almost right word is the difference between lightning and the lightning bug." At the stage of the first draft, if you are finding it difficult to choose the right word, it is fine. In such cases, instead of continuing to struggle, temporarily use the word you feel is appropriate at that time. Later on, as you refine your writing, you can always replace that temporary word with the most appropriate word.
- Select words from the normal speaking vocabulary so that they convey a friendly conversation rather than sounding mechanical or formal. Shun fancy substitutes for everyday words.
- Use words with positive connotations that are also soft, mild, palatable, and non-offensive. Positive words send positive vibes into the reader's mind and will generate a helpful attitude towards you. Converse about negative words is also true. Hence, avoid artificial and angry expressions, camouflaged verbs, or words with negative connotations such as refuse, regret, unfortunately, failure, and nuisance.
- Some people struggle with being able to write more, while others struggle with writing too much and needing to cut it down. Because business writing should be direct and implicit, read over your writing to make sure you've trimmed the fat and cut the fluff. Don't include anything that doesn't need to be there. Even if you have a close relationship with the colleague that you're writing to, it's important to stay professional.
- Avoid verbosity. Avoid wordiness at all levels. Use words sparingly. Waste no words. Make each word count. Read your writing through critical eyes, and make sure that each word works toward your larger point. Cut every unnecessary word or sentence. Verbosity hinders the writing from engaging the reader. "The moment readers feel that a piece

of writing is verbose, they start tuning out," says Garner. If one word can do the job, don't use two words. If two words can do the job, don't use three words. For example, use 'before' instead of 'prior to'. Remove all words that are not performing their real functions. Eliminate padding that doesn't contribute to your meaning. There's no need to say 'general consensus of opinion', for instance, when 'consensus' will do. For instance, write 'The article is verbose' instead of 'The article uses more words than is necessary.' Delete prepositions (point of view becomes viewpoint); replace –ion words with action verbs (use protected instead of provided protection); use contractions (don't instead of do not and we're instead of we are); and swap is, are, was, and were with stronger verbs. Say 'indicates' rather than 'indicative of'. Replace 'ing' wordy be-verb phrases with more direct, simple verbs. This saves the reader's time and facilitates easy comprehension of your message.

- Syllables add up quickly, slowing people down. Of course, stick to idiomatic English. Don't start dropping articles where we would all normally expect them, and do not cut the important words left and right to the extent that it sounds curt or unnatural.
- Redundancy can exist on many levels, from rambling statements to unnecessary repetitions, punctuation, and words that could be replaced by shorter, sharper alternatives; whatever the manifestation, it's bad. Ruthlessly cut words from your first draft as long as you remain faithful to normal, down-to-earth English sounds and rhythms.
- Use the most appropriate words or phrases that emphasise what you want to convey. For example, instead of saying, 'The project was delayed by lockdown.' say, 'The project was delayed by lockdown imposed by the Government of Maharashtra State.' This sentence itself conveys that the delay was beyond your control, even without explicitly saying so. This will avoid the need to explain in the next sentence.
- Give a considered thought to the words and phrases you use in your document and how your reader is likely to receive them, especially if they are negative. If you are respectful and honest, readers will be more willing to accept your message, even if it is negative.
- Avoid boilerplate phrases that degrade your language and suggest lazy thinking.
- Prefer an active voice. Avoid passive voice as much as possible.

- Use sentences that are neither too short nor too long. The reader may register a short, vague sentence in their mind, but they are likely to perceive it as the writer's personal, biased impression. On the other hand, if you make your sentences too long, the reader has nothing to hold on to, and he will get tired of trying. Hence, judiciously decide the length of the sentence. Normally, sentences exceeding twenty words are difficult to comprehend. Also, to avoid monotony, sentence lengths need to vary. Hence, vary the sentence length and aim for an average of twenty words per sentence. Also, don't use the same starting phrases for more than three consecutive sentences. Avoid unnecessary padding, for example,
  - In this connection, it might be observed that …
  - It is important to keep in mind that …
  - It is interesting to note that …
  - It is worthwhile to note that …
  - It is notable that …
  - It should be pointed out that it …
  - It should be remembered that …
- Make your writing fascinating. Avoid trite expressions.
- Creating a good impression requires several ingredients, like selecting the right tone and the right words or phrases most appropriate for conveying the message, the right structuring and organising and many other aspects. However, all it takes is a few ill-conceived words or phrases to make a poor impression.
- Good writing is easy to understand, economical, and straightforward. It doesn't waste the reader's time. In contrast, poor writing is verbose and redundant. The syntax is convoluted and occasionally derails.

5.8 THE FOCUS

- Express your key points clearly. Be relentlessly clear. Put yourself in the reader's shoes to assess your clarity and judge it from the reader's standpoint, not yours. Is your point clear and well-structured? Are the sentences straightforward and concise? However, clarity is a double-edged sword. If you are forthrightly crystal clear, you are sticking out your neck, taking an irreversible position, or recommending an irreversible course of action. Some situations may demand muddy writing in a roundabout manner, leaving room for the reader's views to evolve as events unfold. Hence, strategise your approach depending on the situation.

- Keep in mind the objective of the letter, the addressee, and his organisation all the time, and let these guide what you say and how you say it. Address their needs, both explicitly expressed and implied. For example, if you are replying to a Request For Proposal (RFP), not only address every need expressed in the RFP but also think about the industry, the organisation, its size, and its culture and address other needs so that your submission scores higher than your competitors.
- Maintain intense focus on your reason for writing throughout the letter. Focus on the readers' needs. Let other trivial matters not drift you away from the very purpose of writing.
- Have a feel for natural idioms.
- Business writing is full of industry-specific buzzwords and acronyms. While these terms are sometimes unavoidable and can occasionally be useful as shorthand, they often indicate lazy or cluttered thinking. Jargon doesn't add any value. Throw in too many, and your reader will assume you are on autopilot—or worse, not understand what you're saying. Avoid jargon, business speaks, fancy words, confusing acronyms with uncommon or multiple meanings, and complex words that can cloud your information, though each business may have its own customary style and voice when it comes to its language. A simple and uncluttered writing style goes a long way toward communicating the message to the reader. As much as possible, avoid grandiose writing full of industry-specific buzzwords and acronyms. Otherwise, the reader may not be able to comprehend the document or lose interest in it. Avoid terms like "customisation," "core competency," "impactful," and "incentivise." Writers often mistakenly believe using a big word when a simple one will do is a sign of intelligence. It's not.
- Write so unambiguously that your readers can't possibly misunderstand or misinterpret you. Write with such clarity that the reader finds it easy to comprehend and even enjoyable.
- Grab the reader's attention and hold it. Engage the reader.
- Connect with the reader.

- Connect with the particular reader to connect with a large group of audience. Choose (or create) an intelligent, non-specialist member from the targeted group and focus on writing for that person. Ground your prose by having a particular person in mind who represents the entire group. For example, Warren Buffett kept his sisters in mind when writing to a large community of shareholders of Berkshire Hathaway. Though highly intelligent, his sisters are not experts in accounting or finance. While they understand plain English very well, jargon may puzzle them. This made his writing easy. Thus, by imagining that you are writing for a friend or relative, you can make your writing appealing and pleasing.
- Don't bamboozle or deceive your readers with empty, airy talk.
- Make your tone pleasant, so that your reader will want to spend time with you.
- Prove that you have something valuable to say—valuable from the perspective of readers. Do this quickly. Waste no time in saying that.
- Distil your letter.

5.9 ORGANISING THE LETTER

- Cover only one topic per memo.
- Write the subject of the letter boldly, but concisely.
- Make your letters appealing by making them short and snappy. Use white space effectively. Don't cause strain on the reader's eyes. Provide generous margins, space between paragraphs, etc. Use bold types, italics, bulleted points, short sentences, short paragraphs, indents, titles in colours, etc.
- Outline and organise your paragraphs in order of importance, saving the most convincing or essential information for the end.
- Break paragraphs when new thoughts come up.
- Structure your letters properly.
- Don't use tiny or unusual fonts. Use Times New Roman font size 12, which is much more easily readable than fonts like Edwardian Script.
- Don't use all capital letters. It amounts to shouting at the reader.
- Avoid alphabet soup. Readers find acronyms tiresome. Hence, avoid acronyms like ASAP.

- Use consistent, concise, and descriptive sub-heads.
- Indent sub-information to indicate hierarchy.
- Break up your letter with signposts to lead the reader from section to section and locate the section of interest. Don't make your reader dig for what he wants.
- Instead of reproducing lengthy materials in the body of the letter, consider using attachments as an Annexure or Appendix.
- Don't anaesthetise your reader.
- Don't forget to include attachments, both in letters sent by post, courier, or email. Many times, we click the send button of an email without attachments, and when we realise that attachments were not attached, we send another email with attachments. This doesn't leave a good impression.

5.10 DICTATION

- Realise that dictation is a valuable time-saving skill. While you can write up to thirty words per minute, the dictation output is over 150 words per minute. Hence, get rid of your phobia about dictation and gradually master the art of dictation.
- Start dictation practice with brief letters containing a few sentences. This will give you the confidence to dictate long letters.
- Use a portable Dictaphone freely. Alternatively, use Artificial Intelligence tools. Many smartphones have such tools built in.
- Listen to your tape-recorded voice, and objectively study your speech style for improvements.
- Consolidate your dictation.
- Decide objectives, collect thoughts, and write on a piece of paper before you dictate.
- Have the references ready before you dictate. However, don't procrastinate dictation just because some data or information is not available. Proceed with dictating the first draft, leaving blanks for unavailable information your secretary can collect.
- Spell unusual words for the benefit of your secretary. If you get stuck on some word or idea, say 'something, something' and continue with the dictation and fix it when the draft comes.

- Practice until your dictation skill is sharpened to the stage where the first draft becomes final.

5.11 THE TRUTHFUL SUBMISSION

- Business writing is persuasive because it is evidence-based, clear, and memorable. It should include accurate and relevant information, cut to the chase, but also check that you have your facts and details correct. This is especially true if you're sending out a press release or working on an annual report.
- Include facts while avoiding opinions, generalisations, and broad adjectives to support your pointers. When you provide meaningful, objective details, you are sharing factual information, not just your opinion.
- Never say more than what the occasion demands, and never say less, either. Provide only the information the reader needs—nothing more, nothing less.
- Pave the reader's path with concrete details. Don't push them there with abstract assertions. Give your message some staying power. People don't care about or even remember abstractions in the same way they do specifics. How you write determines its expiration date in the reader's memory.
- Deserve and earn credibility by demonstrating a command of the facts. Establish credibility in the earlier part of the letter. Start with something the reader knows very well or something that is factually correct to the level of cent percent. Once you do this, the reader reads subsequent submissions with a positive bias toward truthfulness, and even if some facts are not so accurate, the reader will look at these facts with a truthfulness bias. However, it should not be construed that the submission of inaccurate facts is advocated.
- Be sincere. Whatever you are writing must sound like what you really mean, and it should come from the bottom of your heart.
- The acceptability of a business letter depends on its neutrality and impartiality. Hence, apart from being truthful, business writing should be neutral and impartial.

- Adopt a balanced approach in your business writing. Business writing should be neither boastful nor weak.

5.12 THE PERSONAL TOUCH

- Provide your contact information for easy reference, even if the addressee already knows it.
- To ensure accuracy, double-check the spelling of names.
- Sign with your full name if you are addressing it as 'Dear Mr. Sunil Patel'. However, if you are addressing him as 'Dear Mr. Sunil, sign with your first name.
- Sign with ink. Don't use a stamp for the signature. Date your documents.
- Regularly send handwritten notes to your customers to strengthen the bond.
- If you are dispatching handwritten notes, use postal stamps rather than franking.
- Avoid printed 'Thank you' notes. Also, don't mass produce 'Thank you' notes; personalise them.
- Write congratulatory notes and deliver them in person with a bouquet. Be generous in your praise and compliments. Do this immediately, without procrastination. However, don't let the passage of time stop you from writing such notes. Also, it is equally or rather more important to pay a visit to your close customer when he or his family member is ill.
- Don't use BCC or NOO (Not On Original). Such endorsements undermine your credibility.
- While drafting, treat the organisation as a living entity (consisting of a group of human beings with emotions) rather than a legal entity. Sound like a human being, not a corporation.
- Avoid writing cold, impersonal letters. Use a warm tone.

5.13 AVOIDING A HOSTILE APPROACH

- Avoid hostility. A hostile or inappropriate tone will undermine your interest. Use a relaxed, watered-down, and professional tone, as if speaking directly. It is possible to deliver almost all kinds of messages, even tough ones, by approaching the reader collegially. No hostility is necessary. By maintaining a civil tone, you can still get results.

- Don't write in anger or frustration. Anger destroys our goodwill. If you can't control your anger, write whatever you want and allow your emotions to vent out. Then, tear off that letter and sit down once again to rewrite it. Don't antagonise the addressee.
- Don't threaten, directly or indirectly. Avoid sarcasm. It diminishes relationship-building, mutual trust, and respect.
- Don't burn bridges. Instead, build an overflowing reservoir of goodwill.
- Avoid quirks that turn readers off.
- The hostile letter need not be replied to by an equally hostile letter. This will add fuel to the fire and start a new series of negative chain reactions. Instead, extinguish the fire and break the chain.
- If you have to deliver rejection, convey this in a very soft and palatable manner. Don't say 'no' directly, but sandwich it subtly between happier elements.
- Don't write anything you would be ashamed of if printed on the first page of the Times of India.

5.14 SUMMARISING

- Summarise each section with a sentence that addresses the five 'Ws' (What, when, where, why, and who) and one 'H' (how).
- Summarise accurately. A good summary is focused and specific.
- The summary should have an impactful punch that the reader can remember.
- Clearly state what action is expected from the addressee. If required, state politely the time frame for the required action. However, convey this in a non-offensive manner. For example, instead of saying, 'Please release outstanding payment on or before the 15th', say, 'We shall be greatly obliged if the outstanding payment is released to us within the next fifteen days or so.'
- Motivate the reader to act and act favourably for you. For this, you may have to meet the reader's needs. You must give them reasons why they will care.
- End the letter with an appropriate complimentary phrase, such as 'Assuring you of our best services always'.

5.15 VETTING THE DRAFT

- The Oxford Dictionary defines vetting as 'examining critically for faults, etc'. Vetting can be self-vetting or external vetting.
- Allow ample time to revise and self-edit your work. Don't believe that your first draft is perfect, or even passable. Every document can be improved. Have a fresh look at the content and structure. Do fine-tuning to sharpen the focus. Most importantly, build time into your schedule for editing and revising. Writing and then reworking your own writing is where the change happens, and it's not quick.
- Don't rashly send anything without proper vetting and improvements. At the same time, don't let an undue obsession with perfectionism delay important business letters.
- Use professional colleagues as a sounding board. Copy your emails or letters to trusted colleagues or peers—both internal and external who are particularly skilled communicators and ask for their feedback. Ask them if there is a better way to convey an idea, and how we can be more succinct. Don't hesitate or feel shy about needing edits. Also, don't be afraid to ask a colleague or friend to edit your work. Welcome their feedback; don't resent it. "Editing is an act of friendship," says Garner. "It is not an act of aggression." Never be afraid to ask for help from someone else who is more comfortable with business writing. It is not one-upmanship. Ask someone to look at examples of your business writing to see if they have constructive criticism for you.
- Accept suggestions gracefully. Seek feedback on the message's clarity and focus, not just language or grammar edits. For example, if you are writing to get approval for additional staff in your department, ask your colleague if he would approve this proposal if he were the approving authority.
- Share the draft at an early stage, when it is still rough. Feedback will shipshape your letter much faster than toiling alone.
- A good writer welcomes good edit ideas and learns from them. A bad writer resents them, seeing it only as a personal attack. A good writer has many ideas, doesn't value them dearly, and willingly shares them with others. A bad writer has a few ideas, and he values them dearly, keeping them close to his chest.

- Foster an environment where edits are freely sought and offered without overtones of petty one-upmanship.
- Never use an ink pen while editing. Use a pencil instead.
- If you are an editor, avoid explaining your edits in person. The recipient may feel shy or uncomfortable and likely to be defencive, and thus, he will find it difficult to accept even good edits. Instead, send the edits through an office person. Look for not only outright errors but also verbose passages. Avoid taking the easy route of saying 'no comments'. Think hard and suggest two good edits per page. Also, don't forget to compliment the writer for his good work. In fact, you should start your comments by complimenting what is good. Once you've done this, the writer will approach edits with a positive mind-set.

5.16 BLACKLIST OF VERBS AND PHRASES

When we are highly aggrieved or frustrated, we are tempted to use certain unpleasant or un-parliamentary words, phrases, or sentences to vent out our feelings. However, regardless of the magnitude of grievances, the severity of provocation, or the level of frustration, a wise person refrains from using such words in both oral and written communication, more so in written communication. Using such a language can never get you results; on the contrary, it may jeopardise your interests and strain your relationships. Respond respectfully, even when someone asks a question with disrespect. Never drag yourself down to the level of the person who is asking you such a question. Maybe he is trying to provoke you. Don't allow him to succeed in his strategy. If you reply disrespectfully, the media may highlight your reply out of context and make headlines out of it. Hence, be extremely careful in your replies, especially when questions are asked disrespectfully. Your skill is to structure your reply in a way that prevents distortion and out-of-context presentation. History will record your reply prominently, not the question to which your reply refers.

Don't use phrases like 'I failed to understand' or 'Your contention is highly erroneous.' or 'You have delayed my payment inordinately.' Such expressions breed ill will. Treat your reader with integrity and fairness, and show that you are willing to meet halfway.

Below is a list of a few words and phrases that we should block or blacklist from our vocabulary and dictionary:

- By no stretch of the imagination …
- It is, least to say, ridiculous to …
- It doesn't make sense to …
- Your comments are absurd and useless …
- I can't tolerate such gross negligence, which …
- If you fail to resolve the issue by the deadline of 3 p.m. on 12th April; be informed that I am going to take up the matter with your Chairperson highlighting your indifferent attitude.
- It is painful to note that my letter has remained unanswered for a month now.

5.17 Do's AND Don'ts

The following list of dos and don'ts reinforces some of the key ideas discussed in the book:

Don'ts	Dos
Point of view	Viewpoint
We provided protection…	We protected …
In view of the fact that …	Because …
You caused a very serious problem.	We are in a challenging situation.
You must agree that I am adequately qualified for the position.	My qualifications in the areas of accounting and customer service meet your job requirements.
"I know that my qualifications are not very impressive, but I will strive hard to meet your expectations if given an opportunity. I hope that you will contact me at …"	"My qualifications make me a suitable applicant for this position. You can reach me at …; I look forward to hearing from you."

You have failed to examine our report.	It appears that perhaps our report has not been examined with due attention because of your busy schedule.
We are surprised to receive your unjustified criticism of our product.	We note your observations on our product, and we are grateful to you for drawing our attention to these observations. We value feedback from our customers.
You didn't read our instructions carefully. That is why your system has been shut down. Hence, you are responsible for this malfunction.	The system may shut down if an installation error occurs.
We never replace equipment damaged because of the customer's gross negligence, even if the warranty period has not expired.	We will be pleased to replace equipment within the warranty period if the same is not damaged because of negligence.
I am writing in response to a number of queries that have been received with regard to recent announcements that Wi-Fi will no longer be complimentary and that use of data beyond a limit of 5 GB will be charged to guests.	We clarify that Wi-Fi shall continue to be provided complimentary up to daily data usage of 5 GB.
I do not understand why you made such discriminatory remarks.	Our organisational policy discourages discriminatory remarks.
I am tired of sending reminders to you for long overdue outstanding payments.	We again draw your kind attention to our outstanding dues, which have remained unpaid for a while.

It is to be noted that a considerable amount of savings has become a reality because we have implemented various planned initiatives for more efficient and effective purchasing procedures. This savings will permit us to improve perquisites for employees.	Savings resulting from streamlining of our purchases will be used to improve employee perquisites.
You have misquoted my last week's telephone talk with you.	I am extremely sorry for the misunderstanding that happened after my last week's telephonic talk. I probably couldn't effectively communicate what I wanted to convey.
As the reasons for the accident are not known as yet, the decision has been taken to suspend production.	Pending investigations, we've decided to suspend production.
You be informed that the GA drawing is now ready for your review.	We are glad to inform you that our GA drawing is ready for your kind review.
You will receive our report ASAP (As Soon As Possible).	We will submit our report to your good self on 7th January.
This applies to all those who have availed of our services in the month of March 2024.	If you availed of our services in March 2024, this applies to you.
Our software cannot open more than ten charts.	Our software can simultaneously open as many as ten different charts, allowing you to view them and make appropriate decisions. This is one of the most important and unique features of our software.

6

BUSINESS WRITING: LAUDABLE STRATEGIES AND AVOIDABLE SYNDROMES

6.1 LAUDABLE STRATEGIES

They say that strategy wins wars, not brute force. The Mahabharata, India's ancient epic, is the best illustration of how tactics may win wars. What do you believe was the primary cause of Abhimanyu's defeat? Was it because twelve Kauvarava warriors ambushed him, creating an extremely unbalanced and unfair twelve vs. one situation? Or maybe it was because Abhimanyu didn't know how to get out of the maze? These are not the real reasons. The critical key factor was Kauvaras's strategy, which led Arjun so far away that he was unable to arrive at the battlefield before dusk. It was nearly impossible to defeat Abhimanyu if Arjun was around. If Arjun had been around, it wouldn't matter if twelve or more warriors had attacked Abhimanyu. Even Abhimanyu's ignorance wouldn't have mattered if Arjun had been present. Strategies are just as important in business situations as they are in warfare.

Each business letter necessitates a distinct, tailor-made strategy, depending on the letter's purpose. However, a few general strategies are universally applicable to various business situations. You need to build up your personal reservoir of strategies. The larger your pool of strategies, the better you'll be able to select the best strategy for the given circumstances. Many other business activities, such as negotiating a business deal, also utilise these strategies. A few of these general strategies are presented below:

6.1.1 The strategy of right timing

Have you observed that even a ten-year-old boy knows when to approach his parents for some favour? He will not ask for additional pocket money from his dad when his dad is in an angry mood. He will wait for the right time to put forth his request. Similarly, he will not approach his mom for permission to go to see a movie with friends when his homework is pending. He will approach his mom only after he completes his homework.

In business situations, it is very important to time your request perfectly. Do you think your customer will entertain your request for approval of a risky or new method for the erection of girders when a major accident took place at the site recently? Or do you think your bankers will sanction your request for additional loans for business expansion when interest on existing loans is overdue? Submitting such a request at the wrong time is likely to result in its rejection. An ill-timed request is likely to fail even if it scores high on other counts. When a request is ill-timed, it doesn't matter whether it is contractually tenable or meritorious, or whether your presentation of the case was the best. These things do not matter when the timing itself is wrong. Hence, you must realise the importance of proper timing in your business situations if you want to succeed in resolving your issues.

6.1.2 The strategy of exploiting leverage

In our personal lives as well as in business situations, we don't get anything worthwhile unless we have a lever in our hands. Without a lever in your hands, you are unlikely to succeed in your attempts. Unfortunately, the world works on this basis. Having a lever in your hands means linking something that your customer wants to something that you want. It means holding back something of critical importance up your sleeve and exploiting it as leverage to get your work done. It means giving a strong message to your customer or vendor that you work on a reciprocating basis. It means making a bold statement that you believe in a win-win strategy. It means making it known to others that you can't be taken for granted. Of course, you need to do this very tactfully, in a soft and palatable manner, without giving your customer the slightest impression that you are blackmailing him. If your customer gets even the slightest hint that you are directly or indirectly blackmailing him, this strategy will not work. Also, your purpose should be bona fide. You should not misuse this strategy.

Suppose, for instance, your builder has sent demand notices to you for interest charges for delays in periodic payments and you have applied for a waiver of these interest charges. The issue is at a stalemate. However, when the flat is ready for possession, the builder can take the stand that he will not give possession until pending interest is paid. This is the lever available in his hand. Similarly, suppose you are constructing a bridge. You have submitted some genuine extra items to your customer that have been pending for several months. Your customer is not entertaining your payment request, though it is legitimate. You apprehend that once the bridge is completed, it will be almost impossible to get this pending payment. In such situations, you can consider deploying this strategy. You can complete the entire bridge except one span and create a situation showing that you are absolutely helpless because of the lack of funds. You keep saying that you are extremely eager to complete the balance, but you don't have funds. You have to convince your customer that you are genuinely facing a financial crisis and that, despite good intentions, you are unable to complete the balance work. If the customer is desperate to open the bridge to traffic, you can treat the last span completion as a lever in your hand to get your genuine payments released. This strategy can yield results if handled tactfully. So what is not possible in normal circumstances becomes possible if you smartly use the lever available in your hand. Remember, levers are always available with you. You only need to think hard, identify the most appropriate lever, and use it strategically for bona fide purposes.

6.1.3 The strategy of ensuring skin in the game

Having skin in the game means having a stake—a financial stake in the game. Unless a stakeholder has a financial stake in the project, his interest will not be serious. His interest in the project will be casual or superficial. Also, the stake should be large enough to hurt him if the project fails. An insignificant stake is not good enough.

If we take an example of a home loan for the construction of a bungalow, no bank provides a home loan unless the owner first invests his own funds to the extent of at least 20%. This ensures that he takes this project seriously. If the bank were to finance the entire 100% cost of the construction, the owner would have no skin in the game. His attitude towards this project would be casual. If the bank is ready to finance 100% of the construction costs, he will take a chance. If the project is successful, it is well and good; if it fails, he has nothing to lose.

When you deal with your vendors, make sure they have some financial stake in the game. Otherwise, they may walk out at any time, especially when things are bad. Since the designer plays a very important role in steel plant projects, in one steel plant project, the owner made the designer firm the equity partner with 1% equity. The owner gave this equity in addition to their usual fees. This completely changed the designer's attitude. Even though the stake was as low as 1%, he acted as if he were the owner of the project. He took the design assignment very seriously and completed it on time. This is despite the fact that almost all steel projects invariably experience delays due to the non-availability of designs and drawings. The owner saved a lot of money, even after giving 1% of the equity to the designer. Hence, when you structure a contract with your vendors, ensure that they have some stake in the game in a suitable form, such as a performance guarantee, liquidated damages, or bonuses.

6.1.4 The strategy of bonus vs. liquidated damages

We happily make stringent provisions in the contract for penalising the contractor for delays, thinking that such negative provisions will avoid delays in the project. No doubt, the penalty provision works as a deterrent, but its effectiveness in avoiding delays is questionable. Punishments don't work even on a ten-year-old boy. If you want him to do some work, incentives like a chocolate bar or additional screen time work wonders.

If you are seriously interested in avoiding delays on the project, consider making a provision for a bonus rather than a penalty, or in addition to a penalty. A well-structured bonus provision can motivate the contractor to expedite the progress. The bonus provision should be generous. It should cover something more than what the contractor would spend to expedite the project. Such provisions have worked wonderfully well on many projects. It is a win-win situation for both the contractor (who earns some more money than he has estimated) and the owner (who saves substantially more than what he has paid as a bonus). This is particularly true for Build-Operate-Transfer (BOT) projects that utilise borrowed funds. BOT projects incur such high interest costs that it is more cost-effective to pay a bonus to expedite project completion and lessen the interest burden. Of course, it is a myth that only BOT projects have interest costs. Even cash contracts have such costs in the form of opportunity costs. This is because you can always make an alternate investment (e.g. a fixed deposit with the bank), and this return, which you are forgoing, is the opportunity cost.

While having a bonus provision in your contract where you are working as a contractor is not in your hands, you can always introduce a bonus provision in your contracts with your vendors and exploit the magical power of this positive provision for mutual benefits.

6.1.5 The strategy of approaching from the top or bottom

Have you observed that even a seven-year-old boy knows who is the right person to approach for a particular type of demand? He puts up some of his demands or requests to his dad, and for some other requests, he approaches his mom, grandmother, or elder sister. He knows who is going to give him additional pocket money, and he strategises accordingly. He will approach his mom if he wants permission to go for a picnic with his friends.

Business situations are no different. To resolve your issues with your customers, you may have to first identify the right person in the hierarchy of the customer's organisation. You can approach either from the top or the bottom. These are two exclusive sets of strategies. Some issues can best be resolved by approaching from the bottom, i.e. approaching the lower-level officers in the hierarchy of the customer's organisation. In some other situations, it pays to approach from the highest level in the customer's organisation. If you adopt the wrong strategy of approaching from the top when approaching from the bottom is required, you will not be able to resolve your issues, however hard you may try. The converse is also true.

The success of this strategy depends on several factors, which include the customer's organisational hierarchy, the stronghold or otherwise of top-level officers in the customer's organisation, the organisational culture of the customer, the types of issues to be resolved, etc. So depending on these factors, you may choose a strategy that is best suited for a given set of circumstances. This applies not only to business writing but also to matters like conducting meetings to resolve issues.

6.1.6 The strategy of opening all cards vs. keeping something up your sleeve

There are two approaches to business writing. In the first approach, you open all your cards in the beginning itself. This means presenting all the arguments in favour of your contention without holding back anything. This type of approach is used when you believe that by opening all cards upfront, you can resolve your issues and avoid back-and-forth correspondence.

As opposed to this, there's another possible approach that advocates not disclosing everything at first, but keeping something up your sleeve. In this strategy, you don't disclose all the points in the first communication. There are situations where you are required to hold back some of the arguments. This also depends on your addressee's nature. Some of the addresses have a habit of finding fault and rejecting the proposal, even if it is meritorious and self-explanatory. They find satisfaction in rejection. When dealing with such a category of addressees, you will have nothing more to say if you have disclosed all your points at the beginning. In such cases, it may be advisable to hold back something up your sleeve and submit the same in the next submission when the first submission is rejected.

6.1.7 The strategy of not closing your options

In business writing, you should never close your options. This is because you never know, with certainty, what your customer prefers or what he may eventually select. Many times, they prefer or select the option that you expected the least. If you have closed your options at the beginning, it becomes very difficult for you to go back to what your customer prefers. Hence, it is a good strategy to keep all options open at the initial stage. Rather than closing all other options and maintaining only one option, allow things to evolve. Let the ideas get crystallised. As things reach the maturity stage, one option may emerge on its own as you discuss the issues with your customer multiple times. Depending on how things pan out, you can zero in on the option that your customer prefers. After all, you are interested only in the end results, not any particular option. Hence, don't get married to one particular option. Adopt a flexible approach and tactfully keep all your options open. Once you understand the customer's perspective, you can confidently gravitate towards their preferred option.

Suppose, for example, you are proposing a rate for an extra item to your customer, and there are, say, three methods of arriving at the rate of this extra item. You strongly advocated the first method, duly highlighting its advantages and projecting it as the only appropriate method to arrive at the rate of an extra item, and you criticised other methods. If your customer insists on using the second method to determine the rate of an extra item, despite your strong advocacy for the first method, it can be challenging to switch back to their preferred method.

6.1.8 The strategy of refraining from giving ultimatums that can't be executed.

In business writing, you should never give 'take it or leave it' kinds of ultimatums, especially to your customers, and even more so if you are not in a position to execute them. Even verbal ultimatums are best avoided, but written ultimatums are strictly prohibited. These types of ultimatums hurt the ego of the customer. Remember, if you are unable to execute your ultimatum, it becomes very difficult for you to go back to the customer. Suppose your customer has not paid your bills for the last six months. You are highly aggrieved by this non-payment. You write a hostile letter to your customer and give him an ultimatum to release the payment within thirty days; failing which, you will stop the work and close down your site establishment. Now, what happens if your customer doesn't release the payment within thirty days or doesn't even bother to reply to you? You had no intention of stopping the work and closing down your site establishment. You merely wanted to threaten your customer. But now you are in a difficult situation. After thirty days, you cannot even write a second letter reminding your customer to expedite the release of payment. You are now in a soup, courtesy of your ill-conceived strategy of giving a time-bound ultimatum.

Similarly, as far as possible, avoid giving such 'take it or leave it' kinds of ultimatums even to your vendors. If you must give ultimatums in peculiar or exceptional situations, ensure they are soft and palatable, leave some escape routes open, and communicate them in a non-offensive manner. For the ultimatum to succeed, it must meet the following four criteria:

1) Frosting on the cake

The other side must have no other choice, or they must have such an investment that they cannot fold their cards and walk away. Hence, the ultimatum must come at the end of the negotiation, never at the beginning. You can't frost a cake unless you bake it.

2) Soft and palatable

The words must never be bitter or offending. Soft ultimatums are palatable because they are simply a statement of your reality. For example, say, "I certainly understand your predicament. Your position is valid, but this is all I have got as per our budget." Although you are, in effect, giving an ultimatum, it doesn't appear as one because it shows empathy, acknowledges the other party's genuineness, reveals your legitimate limitations, and, above all, is soft and palatable.

3) Legitimacy

It is always wise to back up your position with some form of documentation or legitimacy. For example, say, "You deserve what you are asking for. We wish we could give it to you, but this is all we can give as per corporate office policy." Here, the corporate office policy is a legitimate benchmark, and the other party will appreciate this limitation of the project office.

4) Options with a limited menu

Never leave the other side without alternatives. Never say, "It is this or nothing." Rather than providing a 'take-it-or-leave-it' ultimatum, which can be offensive, consider offering limited options. You can structure the situation and give them a couple of options to choose from. Suppose during an interview the candidate is asking for a salary of 3000$ per month. Don't say, "We can give a maximum of 2500$ as a salary and nothing more." This is offensive. Instead, you may say, "You deserve what you are asking for. However, as per the pay scales of our organisation, we can offer something between 2300$ to 2500$. I hope you will appreciate our limitations." Here you structured a range, but you kept the upper range at 2500$ which in any case you were ready to offer. Alternatively, you could propose maintaining a fixed salary range of 1800$ to 2000$, while incorporating a variable component based on performance. If the candidate is confident about his performance, he may opt for variable pay. If so, you will receive additional confirmation regarding the candidate's suitability. This strategy of offering a limited menu is more likely to work than a take-it-or-leave-it type of ultimatum.

6.1.9 The strategy of not burning bridges

Burning bridges means you do something that forces you to continue with a particular course of action, and makes it impossible for you to return to an earlier situation or relationship.

In the good olden days, bridges were made of wood. The soldiers were used to cross the rivers through such wooden bridges, attack the enemy on the other side of the river and return to their territory. While returning, they set fire to the wooden bridge, burning it so that the enemy could not come to their territory and attack them in revenge. Of course, once they burn a bridge, even they can't reach the enemy if they want to attack them a second time.

The strategy of not burning bridges advocates not taking such actions when it is impossible to return to an earlier situation. In business situations, many actions are irrevocable. For example, issuing a final notice of termination is an irrevocable step. Exercise great restraint when invoking such actions. Hence, in business situations, avoid burning bridges. Avoid spoiling the relationships to such an extent that future business becomes impossible.

6.1.10 The strategy of obtaining prior conditional concurrence

If a ten-year-old boy wants to go to see a movie with his friends, he is always apprehensive about getting permission from his mom. Have you observed that if a boy is smart, he will use a different strategy? He approaches his mom without completing his homework. Obviously, his mom will say, "First, you complete your homework." The boy asks, "After I complete my homework, can I go for a movie? The mom replies, "We'll see about that later; first, you complete your homework." Even this reply from the mom is good enough, because indirectly, it is as good as virtual concurrence. If the boy had completed his homework and then asked for permission, would he have gotten it? Probably not.

In some business situations, especially those that are controversial, it is extremely difficult to obtain a customer's concurrence or blessings. In such situations, it pays to voluntarily offer to do something and obtain prior conditional consent from the customer. This, in effect, means that the customer agrees to do something upon you voluntarily doing something. You always obtain such conditional concurrence in advance before fulfilling your part of the commitment.

The customer may agree to this type of conditional concurrence for two reasons. Firstly, on controversial issues, the customer always wants to postpone his affirmative decision to the extent possible. This strategy suits the customer's mentality because it postpones the decision to a future date, and that too is dependent upon you performing your part of the commitment. Secondly, since the concurrence is linked to a future event, which is difficult in the eyes of the customer, he feels even more inclined to agree to such a proposal. The secret to success in this strategy lies in your ability to skillfully link it to the event that the customer thinks is almost impossible or very difficult to fulfill, but you are confident that you can fulfill it. With this strategy, you don't have to insist on such concurrence in writing. Even a verbal assurance or commitment from the customer is sufficient; a subtle or indirect assurance will also do. Once you obtain such a conditional concurrence from your customer, you should diligently perform your part of the commitment.

For instance, let's say you suggest a novel method for girder erection, but your customer is hesitant to approve because it has not been tried before. You can go to your customer and say, "I agree with you, Sir, that we should not take risks. Unless we are sure that this method is workable, we should not try it. I'll try to find out whether anybody else has used this type of method or similar methods in India or even abroad and used them successfully. As you correctly pointed out, we shouldn't employ this method unless it has proven successful elsewhere."

Beautifully worded, this statement implies that we will adopt it if it is successfully implemented elsewhere. Of course, you knew beforehand that such a precedent was available, but as part of your well-conceived strategy, you decided to hold back this information. The customer will readily agree to this offer because he is under the impression that nobody has tried this type of method so far. Once you develop such an understanding with your customer, you don't need to insist on written approval. Now, after a few days, you go to him and tell him that you did a lot of research and found that a similar method was used on a so-and-so project abroad. At this stage, your customer may still say, "What about India? Foreign engineering culture is different. Investigate whether India employs a similar method." Now, this is not merely an ordinary instruction or a statement. This instruction implies that, if Indian precedent is available, he must approve this proposal. Your half of the job is done now because, this way, you have engaged your customer and drawn him into your strategy. The last step in this strategy is to provide him with Indian precedent, and your approval is guaranteed. If you had submitted Indian precedent in the initial stage without obtaining prior conditional concurrence, would it have worked? Probably not. This strategy guarantees success because it involves obtaining prior conditional concurrence and engaging your customers throughout the process. Thus, you can successfully use this strategy for many of your chronic issues, which have been in stalemate for a long period.

6.1.11 The strategy of involving and engaging customers

One manufacturer of crushing plants claimed that his plants are very economical. At the quotation stage, he could have quantified that it would result in, say, 35% savings and enclosed his own calculation sheet justifying this claim. However, he didn't do this. Instead, this smart manufacturer asked his customer for an appointment to make a presentation. During the presentation, he came up with a blank Excel sheet in which all the data was to be filled in. He kept asking questions like, "What is the cost of boulders in your project?" "What is the rate of diesel?" "What is the manpower cost?" etc. He went on feeding all these answers into the Excel sheet and arrived at % savings in a live environment in front of his customers.

If he were to submit his calculations, his customer would have questioned 35% savings and made several comments, like, your assumptions are incorrect, your calculations are theoretical, there are lots of exaggerations, and so on.

However, can the customer make such comments now? He can't. This is because he provided input for calculations and was fully involved in them. Now, he owns these calculations. He will even defend the same if his boss comments. What caused such a vast change in the customer's attitude? The strategy of involving and engaging the customer in calculations worked beautifully well. When you involve your customer and engage him in dialogue, you are acknowledging his importance. You are valuing his knowledge and wisdom. You are respecting him. All of these factors lead to dopamine spikes, making him own the calculations. Now, it is no longer a unilateral calculation by the manufacturer.

6.1.12 The pre-emptive strategy

Imagine two siblings: a boy (five years old) and his sister (three years old) are playing in the children's room, and their parents are watching TV in the living room. Suddenly, the girl starts crying profusely. Immediately, the boy rushes to the living room, and suo-motto tells his parents, "I haven't pushed her. She fell down on her own." Look at the beautiful strategy of this five-year-old boy. He anticipated that, listening to his sister's crying, his parents would come rushing to the children's room and start scolding him or even start beating him, presuming he had pushed his sister and made her cry. In order to forestall and preempt such a situation, the boy smartly adopts this beautiful strategy as a precautionary shield. Of course, the parents can still scold him, but the boy has at least succeeded in forestalling a knee-jerk reaction from the parents. Now that he has pleaded his innocence in advance, it will be rather difficult for his parents to start scolding him instantly. Now, before taking any action, parents will at least ask the daughter what exactly happened. Such a situation is quite familiar, and many of us must have observed this kind of pre-emptive tactic from a young child in our family or the neighbourhood. This boy, when he grows up, may continue to use this strategy internally in his organisation or externally with his customers or vendors.

The pre-emptive strategy essentially consists of taking suo-motto action in advance to prevent or dilute some precipitative action you are anticipating from the other party. Filing an application in court for anticipatory bail is a good example of the pre-emptive strategy. Similarly, suppose, based on some inside information, you anticipate that your customer will issue a show-cause notice to you for your project, which is running substantially behind schedule, and the current rate of progress is so poor that a time overrun is inevitable. In that case, you may adopt this strategy. You may write a suo-motto letter to your customer explaining the whole situation. You may write about the reasons beyond your control that resulted in delays in the project, as well as the steps you are planning to take to expedite progress. This may dilute the situation to some extent, if not completely. Of course, you can't completely rule out the possibility of your customer still issuing a notice, but at least you've succeeded in making this task somewhat difficult for them. Also, this will at least give you some time to expedite the progress, and maybe if the progress improves, the topic of show-cause notice itself might become redundant.

You can also apply this strategy internally. You may inform your boss that the customer is contemplating issuing a show-cause notice. This has two advantages. Having pre-informed him, he won't react impulsively when the show-cause notice is actually received. Also, he will appreciate James Bond's qualities in you because you have a system in place to get intelligence inputs before the event takes place. You can go even one step further and request that your boss address a pre-emptive letter to the Chairman of the customer. If this letter helps to stop the show-cause notice, you praise your boss and give him all of the credit. If it fails, the blame will not be apportioned to you in any case.

Suppose a fire breaks out in one residential flat of a multi-story building because of negligence by one of the members of society. This caused a lot of damage to the owners of neighbouring flats. The defaulting member anticipated that neighbours and other members of society would take action against him. To preempt such action from fellow society members, the smart defaulting member sends a beautifully worded message to all society members, which reads as follows:

"Hello Everyone,

Firstly, many thanks to you all for helping us during this unfortunate event of fire. I am blessed to have neighbours like … and … to be there and make the best use of a fire extinguisher. Special thanks to Mr… who installed the extinguisher a few years ago and maintained it in working condition. Also, the security guards, Mr… and … came in at the right time.

The cause of the fire is unknown, but my daughter and wife switched off the mains as soon as they saw it. They also alerted the neighbours immediately, who came for help instantly and could control the fire just in time.

Thanks to Mr… and many others from our society who reached out on time and controlled the situation. What saved us was that extinguisher on the floor and some really brave efforts by alert neighbours, society members, and security guards.

In the end, what mattered the most was that everyone was safe.

Thank you all, and God bless this wonderful society."

After this message, it becomes very difficult for any of the members of the society to attack the defaulting member. This is a beautiful example showing how we can try to forestall some potentially adverse situations by deploying a pre-emptive strategy.

6.1.13 The strategy of voluntary commitment

In certain business situations, it is advisable to voluntarily commit something to the customer, even if you are not required to do so in normal circumstances. This strategy involves making such voluntary commitments, which are then followed by statements specifying what the customer is required to do, thereby indirectly obtaining a follow-up commitment from the customer.

Suppose, for example, you are submitting a tender for a project in a foreign country. You can state, "All expenses which are incurable in India pertaining to the mobilisation of manpower from India shall be borne by us." At first glance, you may feel such a statement is unwarranted. Your initial reaction would be, why should I make such a statement on my own?

However, such a voluntary statement is necessary so that in the next sentence, you can state, "All expenses incurable in your country pertaining to the mobilisation of manpower from India shall be borne by you."

If you had not voluntarily made the first statement but just made the second statement, the second statement is unlikely to be accepted. But by voluntarily committing what you will do through the first statement, you made acceptance of the second statement almost guaranteed. When presented in this manner, customers are likely to accept your proposal. Thus, in such situations, it pays to go out of your way and make a voluntary commitment.

6.1.14 The reverse strategy

In one L.S. contract for the construction of an Electric Grid Control Centre, the scope of the work also included the construction of telecom towers, the quantity of which was specified as 500 m. The smart owner issued a revised drawing, R1, indicating an increase in the telecom tower quantity to 750 m. Immediately, the contractor reacted and asked for extra payment for 250 m of additional telecom towers, though it was a L.S. contract. The owner agreed and even signed an amendment to pay extra.

Later, the owner issued R2 of the drawing, which showed the quantity of telecom towers as 150 m. Having signed the amendment, can the contractor refuse to pay the rebate for the 350 m of the tower he is not executing? Obviously, not. The owner trapped the contractor with his smart strategy. If the owner hadn't adopted this strategy, the contractor would have refused to pay a rebate for a reduction in quantity, with the contract being L.S.

Similarly, in yet another contract on foreign soil, the customer asked for a broad break-up of prices into labour charges, local materials, and imported materials. Assuming that the customer will never procure imported materials themselves, the contractor intentionally gave a skewed break-up as follows, keeping the total price the same.

	Estimated Price	**Quoted Price**
Labour charges	1.1 million $	1.1 million $
Local materials	2.8 million $	1.3 million $
Sub-total	**3.9 million $**	**2.4 million $**
Imported materials	4.5 million $	6.0 million $
Total	8.4 million $	8.4 million $

Surprisingly, the smart customer took the gamble of procuring imported materials himself. The poor contractor had to accept the contract at 2.4 million $ against his estimate of 3.9 million $ resulting in a loss of 1.5 million $.

6.1.15 The strategy of respecting trade customs and practices

Always respect the customs and practices prevailing in your trade. If you violate such customs and practices, you are likely to face difficulties at a later date when you administer the contract.

Suppose you are submitting an offer to a builder to construct residential buildings based on the per-square-foot rate on the slab area. You assume and specify that all the slab areas will be considered for measurement, including balconies. However, industry trade practice dictates that the total area does not include balconies in full, but rather multiplies them by a factor of 0.5. This makes sense because building balconies is less expensive than building a living room or a bedroom. Balconies have no walls, and obviously, to that extent, they will cost less than a living room. It is more prudent to respect this trade practice and work out your rate, assuming that balconies will be paid at 50%. If you ignore this practice and submit your offer considering that the balconies will also be paid in full like any other room and quote a lower rate, you are likely to have difficulties at a later date during the administration of the contract. Citing the trade practice, someone in the hierarchy of customers will measure the balcony area at 50% instead of the full area.

6.1.16 The strategy of exploiting deadline pressure

The deadline pressure works wonders. If your customer has some deadlines that are very critical for him, you can get an unimaginable amount of concessions or help from your customer, which would be almost impossible to get in normal circumstances. This is also true for vendors. If you are aware of the deadlines of your customers or vendors, you can deploy this strategy. Suppose your customer has a deadline to commission the project, which is very critical for him. In such cases, he will be extremely eager to take over the project from you and commission it. He will start giving you concessions after concessions in order to fulfill his commissioning target. He will ignore many of the pending items. However, the converse is also true. Suppose you have completed your project, but your customer is not keen on taking over because some other interconnected projects are not yet completed. In such situations, you will not be able to hand over the project, however hard you try. He may point out hundreds of minor defects and make you rectify those defects. Once you rectify these defects and approach him again for taking over, he will find another set of defects and make you rectify those. He does this because he has no deadline pressure.

Similarly, suppose your vendor is in desperate need of funds because his account is likely to become non-performing if he doesn't deposit overdue interest with his bankers. In such a scenario, he may offer you an unimaginable discount on pending payments. He might have submitted genuine claims, but in such a situation, he may be ready to settle the same at a much lower amount. So, it always pays to know what the deadlines are for your customers or vendors. Once you know the deadlines, you can plan a suitable strategy to exploit the deadline pressure.

6.1.17 The strategy of strengthening the hands of your customers

In business situations, you have to often strengthen the hands of your customers. Many times, even if a customer wants to extend some help or make a concession to you, he may be helpless and cannot do so unless you strengthen his hands. This is because the officer who wants to extend some help to you is accountable in his organisation. He has to justify his decisions to his superiors in his organisation. To satisfy this requirement, you may have to strengthen the hands of your customers by giving them some undertaking or some commitment. Apart from customers, this strategy can be used even with your vendors or bankers.

For example, suppose you have procured a Bank Guarantee (BG) from a bank by depositing an amount equivalent to, say, 50% of the BG value as collateral in the form of a Fixed Deposit (FD). Normally, this FD will be released only when you return the original BG to the bank duly discharged by your customer. However, although the validity of the BG has expired and even the claim period has also expired, you are unable to get the original BG back from your customer. And you still want your FD to be released. The bank manager may help you by releasing this FD if you've got a good business relationship with the bank. However, you may have to strengthen the hands of the bank manager by providing an undertaking to the bank, if he so desires. Because you need some concession with respect to the normal practices prevailing in the industry, you should not hesitate to give an undertaking. If you take the stand, 'Why should I give an undertaking?' you may not be able to get your FD released.

6.1.18 The strategy of reinforcing your contention by a third-party opinion

We may blow our own trumpet, but what matters most is the third-party opinion. When the issues involved are highly controversial, our own opinion is not good enough. This opinion will be considered biased because we are an interested party. However, if we can supplement our contention with opinions from a third party, it will carry a lot of weight. On technical issues, opinions from reputed institutes like IIT work wonders. Similarly, an opinion from a retired judge, a reputed advocate, an expert chartered accountant, etc. carries lots of weight. Of course, this needs to be discussed with the customer in advance before obtaining a third-party opinion. In meetings, we may raise this topic and put up a poser, 'How about taking some third-party opinion?' If the customer's response is positive, put up a second question, 'Whose opinion should be obtained?' and, in the same breath, suggest a couple of names keeping control of the conversation in your hand.

For example, if a structure you designed fails, no amount of justification from your side will satisfy the customer. But if you submit a third-party opinion, after a prior concurrence from the customer, it will serve the purpose.

6.1.19 The Bottom Line Up strategy

One of the best ways to make your business writing clearer and more direct is to use the Bottom Line Up (BLU) Strategy. This means stating your main point, recommendation, or request first and then adding supporting details and evidence. It means you shorten the time to value, i.e. help readers get something out of your writing as soon as possible. Using the BLU strategy helps readers understand the main point right away without getting lost in details. And it makes your content easier to scan and digest. In this strategy, you begin your writing with the most important information at the very top. For example, 'We need your feedback on the report by the 15th of this month.' By stating this at the beginning of the letter, the reader knows what is expected of him without getting lost in the details. Similarly, say, 'Our product can help you save 30% on your energy bills.' Here's how:' With this statement at the beginning, the reader keeps this context in mind while reading subsequent text, and he is in a better position to appreciate the reasons for such savings. To take another example, 'Revenue increased by 15% last quarter thanks to these three strategies:'.

Many times, the writing style and structure that were taught in school don't work well in the business world. "One of the great diseases of business writing is postponing the message to the middle part of the writing," says Garner. By succinctly presenting your main idea first, you save your reader's time and sharpen your argument before diving into the bulk of your writing. When writing longer memos and proposals, Garner suggests stating the issue and proposed solution at the top of the first page, and that too in no more than 150 words. Acquire a knack for summarising. If your opener is no good, then the whole piece of writing will be no good either. When David McCombie began working as a management consultant at McKinsey & Company, he immediately realised that the writing style he'd honed at Harvard Law School wasn't well suited for executive-level communication. "It was the structure of my arguments," David says. "I was receiving feedback that I needed to get to the point more quickly. With legal or academic writing, you're going to generally start with building up the case and put the main point all the way at the end. But in business communication, it's best to start with your conclusion first."

6.1.20 The fall-back strategy- A Brahmastra

In construction companies, whenever a new project starts, the labour contractors, popularly known as Piece Rate Workers (PRWs) are called to the Head Office to discuss the rate directly with the Director. Typically, a PRW is mostly an illiterate person. However, you will be amazed to see that they possess quite a good knowledge about the analysis of labour rates. They know the productivity of labour, the size of the labour gang required for a particular task, etc. and above all, they have mastered the art of negotiations.

The discussions about rates go on for three to four hours. Throughout the discussions, the PRW will stand in front of the Director and will not sit in the chair, despite repeated offers to sit down. That is how he wants to show his respect to the Director.

Once the rates are arrived at, he will make a closing statement in vernacular language, which is equivalent to; "Sir, I am an illiterate person from a small village. I can't read or write. I can't even sign. I will put my thumb impression on whatever you say, but, Sir, if I lose money, I will come back to you." What a masterstroke from this illiterate (?) PRW! With one stroke, he has very smartly undone and nullified what was discussed during the last three to four hours. As part of his strategy, he is not forcefully insisting on his own rate directly, but he is maintaining his upper hand by saying that I am accepting whatever rate you are offering me. Again, what a fantastic strategy from this illiterate guy! As a strategy, this is much better than insisting on a few rupees extra in the unit rates at this stage. Instead, he is keeping a safety valve open, which he can operate anytime he wants. If he insists on his rates, the safety valve will obviously become unavailable. Of course, do you think that during the long discussions, the PRW would not have indirectly influenced the rate that the Director had arrived at? He is too smart to miss such opportunities. Definitely, he must have influenced the arriving of rates by the Director favourably from his point of view by giving intelligent inputs like the productivity of labour etc.

Adoption of such a strategy is not limited to PRWs only. I saw the Chairman of one large contracting organisation adopting a similar strategy while negotiating a multi-billion $ contract in North Africa. At the end of a long negotiation meeting, he made a similar closing statement to the Chairman of the owner's organisation. He said, 'Sir, I don't understand the Arabic language. I am blindly signing whatever contract you are giving me, but I will come back to you in case there is something unforeseen. I am sure you will bail me out in such an eventuality.' The strategy is similar to what PRW was using. If there was a difference, it was in the mode of travel they used: PRW travelled by train to attend the meeting; the Chairman travelled by his private jet! The other difference is that the Chairman is using a bit of sophisticated language. Whereas PRW says that he will come back if he loses money, the Chairman is not so vocal in his expression, and instead, he says I will come back to you if there are unforeseen circumstances; the effect is the same in either case.

Once, I was talking to this Chairman and praised his strategy. He said, "Gentleman, you just can't venture into unknown territory overseas unless you have a Godfather with you who can bail you out in case of difficulties." What a great piece of advice!

This strategy is like having a Brahmastra in your hands. You can use this when all other strategies fail. Its success is guaranteed.

6.2 AVOIDABLE SYNDROMES

6.2.1 I-am-OK-you-aren't-OK syndrome

Many people suffer from the 'I'm-OK-you-aren't-OK' syndrome. This syndrome is an aggressive philosophy focused on self-superiority (whether real, perceived, or self-proclaimed), represented by one of the four quadrants of the transactional analysis matrix. 'I'm-OK-you-aren't-OK' thinking develops when people think only they are worthy and others are not. They suffer from a superiority complex. They self-certify themselves as OK and label the rest of the world as not OK. They believe that the fault always lies with the rest of the world. If something is wrong, it is with others, not with me. This aggressive philosophy can result in arrogance or disrespect for authority. They may also develop a perfectionist streak to prove their self-proclaimed superiority.

TRANSACTIONAL ANALYSIS MATRIX

Permutations		Quadrant	Life position	Pre-dominant characteristics
I am okay	You are okay	I	The healthy position	Attitude of openness, honesty and trust
	You aren't okay	II	The one-up position	Attitude of anger, disgust and disdain over designated inferiors with self-proclaimed superiority

I am not okay	You are okay	III	The one-down position	Depressive attitude with lack of self-confidence and feeling of having been victimised
	You aren't okay	IV	The hopeless position	Attitude of futility and frustration

When your customer suffers from this syndrome, he may overpower all of his contractors, mistaking his positional power for greater societal worth. He doesn't respect others' viewpoints and is insensitive to others' feelings. He will dictate or force his views on others and expect others to change their viewpoints, actions, and behaviour. When we assume another person is OK, wants to do the right thing, or has good intentions, honest mistakes are accepted. However, when we hold the aggressive view that others are not OK, we regard their human errors as the result of their inferiority or an act of malice. You must treat such a customer tactfully by praising him and nurturing his ego.

6.2.2 My-way-or-highway syndrome

My way or the highway is an ultimatum, meaning you either fulfill my requirements or do not participate. Some people believe that only their viewpoint or way of doing things is right. Such people don't respect others' views. They insist people adopt only their way of doing things and not any other way. They are not sensitive to others' feelings. They suffer from a superiority complex. This is a highly autocratic approach. Since their ultimatums are threats, others have no choice but to fall in line.

6.2.3 I-told-you syndrome

Many of us suffer from I-told-you syndrome. If something untoward happens, we retrospectively say, "I told you this would happen, but you never listened to me." There are a couple of variants of this syndrome. In its simplest form, one category of people makes the above statement and gets satisfaction merely by uttering it. Other categories of people are so egoistic that they even go to the extent of sabotaging just to prove that what they said was right. This satisfies their ego. They want to show that they have a sixth sense and can predict the future. In yet another variant, people say, 'I told you' even when they have never told you so!

While we should avoid this syndrome, we should be aware of people suffering from it and have an appropriate strategy to deal with it.

6.2.4 Self-praising syndrome

Avoid self-praising in both oral and written communication—especially in written communication. Even if you need to praise yourself in some exceptional situations, you must prefix the same with phrases, like 'Not bragging but…' or 'Not boasting myself but …'.

Additionally, you need to be aware of your business associates who are suffering from this syndrome. In fact, you should identify those business associates who crave dopamine spikes. If deemed appropriate, you may exploit this weakness of your business associates to your advantage in getting your work done. So long as you use this for bona fide purposes and don't misuse it, it is legitimate to get your work done by causing dopamine spikes, especially because they love it.

6.2.5 Self-congratulating syndrome

Many people love self-congratulating. They suffer from a superiority complex. They love bringing their achievements to the limelight, however small they might be. Some of them self-congratulate themselves directly, in no uncertain terms, and expect you to respond with a congratulatory note. Some other people indicate this indirectly and present the data, information, or their achievements in such a way that provokes you to send them a congratulatory note. Regardless, their goal is to receive a congratulatory note from you. Don't disappoint them. Send them a well-written congratulatory note as soon as possible. Use superlative words and phrases. Don't be a miser while praising.

Your vendors or customers, as well as your employees, do it. Don't disappoint them, either. However, if your employees have to resort to demanding congratulatory notes even for their genuine achievements, it shows the failure of HR policy. A wise boss is prompt in congratulating his employees. He is always alert. He doesn't wait for a self-congratulatory letter from his staff.

6.2.6 Self-protecting syndrome

Many people have a strong desire to protect themselves. They don't want to get into trouble in the future. They build a strong cage of defence around themselves. They do this in both written and oral communication. They are so proficient at doing so that it is almost impossible to catch them. The boss will never be in a position to apportion blame to them because they have proactively protected themselves from any possible blame from all angles. We should be aware of such people.

If the writer is building a case for escaping responsibility in the future, he may aim at something other than getting the point across. For example, if interest rates vary widely, the writer wants to protect himself. If he is suffering from the self-protecting syndrome, his entire focus will be on how to save his skin in case the interest rates vary widely with respect to what he has assumed. He is so obsessed with the need to save his skin that he will first start by assuming the scenario that is safest for him, though it may not be the right thing to do. Secondly, he will smartly build a safety net around himself to protect him in the future. The productivity of such people will be too low because they take the safest decisions (safest from the viewpoint of saving their skin) and spend a lot of their time building the safety net around themselves.

7

HOW TO FOSTER ENRICHING BUSINESS RELATIONSHIPS

*I*n our personal and professional lives, we interact with family, friends, neighbours, colleagues, bosses, customers, vendors, and others. The time efficiency and spiritual maturity with which we conduct these interactions not only dictate our personal and professional success, but they also affect the quality of our lives. Relationships with customers rank second in a golden quadrilateral of relationships, which includes spouse, customer, boss, and secretary/staff. Of course, all relationships are important, including friendships, but these four relationships play a large role in your professional success as you spend the most time in these four relationships.

It's very hard to build a relationship merely with correspondence, emails, letters, bullet points, or presentations. Nowadays, we extensively use WhatsApp messages instead of making a voice call. However, the frequency of our text messages doesn't necessarily equate to building intimacy or nurturing relationships. These devices and apps are just tools for communicating with one another. And when we use them, we often seem to run on autopilot. Relationship building is a complex and time-consuming process. It requires a heavy dose of voice calls, video calls, official interactions, official meetings, personal interactions, personal meetings, social meetings, and so on. Though formal letters can fortify business relations and convey credible insights and appreciation, when you communicate after building relationships with someone, it changes the way people react to what you are saying. If you have developed an enriching relationship with your customer, he will read your communication with a positive bias. It encourages him to linger. It has a subtle impact on his decision-making process. Get the relationship right, and you won't have to work so hard on the cold logic of what you are selling.

Relationships with customers are important in all businesses, but they are all the more important in the construction and infrastructure industry. This is because a lot depends on the discretionary power of the customer in the capacity of an Engineer-in-charge or Team Leader as a consultant. In a typical construction project of, say, 100 million dollars, the relationships can make a whopping difference of plus or minus 10 million dollars in the bottom line of the contractor, depending upon the two extreme ends of the relationships. However, this is a gross understatement if the project is on a BOT basis. It can have a devastating impact on BOT projects. If relationships are not good, it can even lead to losing a case in arbitration. In normal circumstances, once an arbitration process starts, the dispute is treated as handed over to a tribunal of impartial persons. The tribunal's role is to adjudicate the dispute impartially, and their superior position enables them to do so. This is because while the minds of both parties are clouded by emotions, prejudices, or biases that might have developed between the two parties during the project execution, the tribunal has no such old baggage. Moreover, both parties have a financial stake in the game. Hence, once arbitration starts, the role of both parties is limited to presenting their case to the tribunal, and all channels of communication must stop. Both parties must step back and assume an extremely passive role. However, if the relationships are at the lowest level, the hostile approach of the customer can continue to extend even after the commencement of arbitration or even after the publication of the award and beyond in subsequent legal battles. In short, relationships with customers are indeed worth a billion dollars.

7.1 CUSTOMER-FIRST PHILOSOPHY

- Treat the customer like a king. Translate this slogan into concrete actions rather than lip service. The customer is the very reason for the existence and survival of your organisation. If your customer goes to your competitor, your organisation's very existence will be endangered.

- Understand the customer. Understand his feelings and emotions. He has unlimited needs, desires, wants, and aspirations, but he has limited resources or pretends to have limited resources. He looks for value for each dollar he spends. He wants to hire the country's number one contractor, but he is willing to pay only what the smallest contractor is asking for. He is always in a hurry, or he pretends to be in a hurry. A project that, in normal circumstances, needs a minimum of thirty-six months, he wants to be completed in thirty months. (This is despite the fact that the same project might have taken five or six years to reach the stage of tendering!) Similarly, if a report requires three working days for its preparation, he wants it in twenty-four hours. He wants you to rectify defects not only during the contractual Defect Liability Period but also beyond that. Hence, the organisation that provides value to the customer, satisfies his even rather unreasonable demands, and serves him in a time-efficient manner is likely to win the customer's heart sustainably.
- In addition to expecting the best product quality, customers also look for the best service. The concept of quality is not limited only to the quality of the product or service, but is quite comprehensive and starts with how your telephone operator answers the customer's call. Other things being equal, customers will go where they can get better service. Hence, provide the best service to your customers.
- Satisfy the present and future needs of the customer and continually enhance his satisfaction. Delight him.
- Sell certain satisfaction. Don't sell a product.
- Don't contradict the customer on facts. Acknowledge and accept the customer's statement, tender an apology if required, and then give convincing logic to justify your stand. This will give you a platform to bounce back aggressively when you have the upper hand. For example, if a customer complains that your product has failed on the first day itself, don't say this is impossible. If you contradict him, he will take an even more aggressive stand. Instead, acknowledge his statement and politely say, "We regret the inconvenience caused to you on account of the failure of our product on the very first day. We are grateful to you for drawing our attention to this failure. We have been supplying this product for the last ten years. In this ten-year history, such an incident

has taken place for the first time. We are deputing our representative to your place to investigate the root causes behind such an unprecedented failure. Once again, thanks a lot for your valued feedback." The reply, as stated above, will change his attitude towards you. If he was biased against you, he would reconsider it now. If he had exaggerated his comments, he would feel guilty now. Thus, you can win your customer's heart even with a humble and submissive approach; you don't need aggression. In fact, aggressive knee-jerk reactions may spoil your case.

- Don't defend something just for the sake of defending it.
- Drive your organisation into a customer-centric mode rather than an internally oriented one. Rise above inter-departmental issues and pay attention to customer requirements.
- Everyone in your organisation should sing from the same hymn sheet as far as the external world or customers are concerned. When you have several teams or offices, getting everyone to feel and act like they work for the same organisation can be a tough job. More importantly, customers do not like inconsistency, and your brand is dead without consistency. Suppose a person who has made the first presentation or sales pitch to the customer is not available for the second presentation. In that case, the new person should carry the first presentation forward the same way the first person would have made it. Customers like organisational continuity. While you work on building the culture and processes that bind growing businesses together, use a single compelling voice with the external world—a voice that properly captures the personality of your business and its unique culture. Your history, motivation, and way of working are at the heart of what you do, and they can make you stand out. It's part of what your organisation is. It's how people recognise your organisation. It's how you get things done. Get your business voice right, and people will notice and remember you. Your customers, as well as your people, will hear the unity.
- A business that writes what it thinks is a business that understands relationships.
- If you don't have the bottle or the skills to write it like how it should be, find the people in your organisation who can. Once you do this, you just might find that it catches on, and everyone starts writing like a professional writer. Similarly, look for individuals with authentic voices

who can speak the dialect of your business. Get them to help convey news and ideas in ways that people will understand, appreciate, and remember. It is no surprise that the World Economic Forum emphasised how soft skills, such as verbal and written communication skills, rank among the top ten skill sets sought after by employers.
- Never take your internal differences to customers. Don't speak ill about any of your colleagues in front of customers. Don't settle your scores on the pitch of customers.
- Repeat customer orders are one of the most appropriate measures of organisational excellence.

7.2 RESPECT THE CUSTOMER

Respect your customers. This applies to both oral and written communication. The letters to the customers should be full of respect and courteousness. Respect and courtesy should drip from each sentence, each paragraph, and each page. Even if this introduces some fat in the text, it is fine because respect is of paramount importance. Place the recipient on the elevated pedestal. Nurture his ego. Value your customers; after all, they are signing your cheques. However, avoid hyper-formality.

The following examples of Dos illustrate the ways of showing respect to customers in written communication:

Don'ts	Do's
Reference your letter no. ...	We acknowledge with thanks the receipt of your letter no...
We would like to have a meeting with you on Thursday, 6th January at 11 am.	We request you to kindly spare some time from your busy schedule and grant us an appointment to have a meeting with your good self at your kind convenience.
This has reference to the meeting held on...	We wish to thank your good self for the kind courtesy extended to the undersigned during the meeting held on ...
Refer to clause no. ...	We draw your kind attention to clause no. ...

A time extension of ... days be granted.	We request you to kindly grant a time extension of ... days.
We totally disagree with your statement that ...	We respectfully beg to differ with your statement that ...
Your contention is highly erroneous, patently illegal, and bad in law.	We respectfully beg to differ with your contention. In our humble opinion, this contention is probably not in line with the provisions of the law.

Offering something beyond the customer's expectations or providing a value-added service are other ways to show respect.

7.3 TRUST: THE CORNERSTONE OF RELATIONSHIPS

- A commitment builds hope, but when you keep it, you build trust.
- Trust means giving someone the power to break your heart, but having faith that he will not do so.
- Trust is the glue that holds relationships together. Love and respect form the foundation of trust. Trust is a cornerstone of our future success. Trust is the foundation of all relationships—personal, business, and social. Trust is the soul of relationships. Relationships that are based on a sound foundation of trust live long, weathering out storms of misunderstandings, unintended or otherwise.
- With trust, every silence is understood. But without trust, every word could be misunderstood.
- People conduct business with people they trust.
- Default to trust. Don't pre-judge someone guilty unless proven. Even the judiciary can't do this.
- Don't spy on any relationships. It shows a lack of trust and breeds dishonour. When you don't trust someone, can you expect him to act honourably? First, deserve it, and then seek trust. Trust a man, and he will trust you. Trust begets trust.
- Earn trust from others by demonstrating your honesty, integrity, and sincerity. There is no such thing as a minor lapse of integrity. Integrity has to be cent percent. Show zero tolerance for those who compromise

their integrity. Of course, before doing that, you have to lead by example and maintain your integrity at a cent-percent level. Therefore, make it a habit to have integrity in your life that will stand up to any scrutiny.

7.4 DEVELOP TRANSFORMATIONAL RELATIONSHIP

- Don't limit your relationship to a particular transaction. This is a selfish approach. Don't be under the impression that your customer will not notice this. They do notice this, though they may choose to remain silent or convey it indirectly to you or sarcastically at times.
- Develop a transformational relationship rather than a transactional relationship. Transformational relationship means developing relationships unselfishly. It focuses on developing a personal rapport with your customer. It enhances sympathy, empathy, and trust between you and your customer. It is developed with a long-term horizon in mind. It doesn't focus on results or benefits. When you develop a transformational relationship, the benefits will come on their own as a by-product. If you want to develop a transformational relationship with your customers, establish a personal equation with them. Apart from official communication, open up channels of personal or informal communication. Open an emotional account with them. Talk to them frequently. Meet them on social occasions. Even if there are no issues to discuss or no formal agenda, make time to meet them. Send them 'Good Morning' messages. Greet them at festivals. Congratulate them when they achieve milestones or promotions. Invite them to lunch or dinner. Know their favourite restaurants and their food preferences. Learn about their other interests. Know the movies they watch. Know their political views. Send them messages that are relevant to their taste. If he is suffering from, say, diabetes, forward relevant messages pertaining to diabetes. Regardless of the value or usefulness of such messages, it registers in his mind that someone is caring for my health. Visit the hospital if your customer or a family member is hospitalised. Regularly obtain feedback from them. Enquire about how your organisation meets their expectations and what more needs to be done to continually enhance their satisfaction. Contrary to this, a transactional relationship focuses only on a specific transaction. Once

the transaction is completed, you discontinue your relationship until when the next transaction is required to be carried out. It focuses on short-term objectives. However, when you develop a transformational relationship, each meeting with your customer takes your relationship to the next level. Once a relationship is developed along these lines, you can get your work done with ease. It is highly rewarding. It can fetch you repeat orders from your customers.

7.5 IS WINNING ARGUMENTS MORE IMPORTANT THAN RELATIONSHIPS?

- Cultivate the habit of showing tolerance for the feelings of others. We are all entitled to have our opinions and beliefs. Hence, respect different shades of opinion. You don't have to agree with everybody in this world, and everybody doesn't have to agree with you, but that doesn't mean you are right or they are wrong. Be open to all points of view, but remain detached.
- Relinquish the need to defend your viewpoint. Similarly, relinquish the urge to convince others to accept your viewpoint.
- Eliminate the desire to be right and win the argument. This applies to all relationships, and more so with customers.
- Discussion is an exchange of thoughts and knowledge. Promote it. The argument is an exchange of ego and ignorance. Avoid it. Focus on what is right rather than who is right. Is winning an argument worth it if you lose peace of mind? Value relationships more than winning an argument.
- Keep your personal feelings, prejudices, and egos right out of the picture. This way, you will get along with others easily. Each time we kill our ego, we rise spiritually.
- Disagree tactfully. Request the other person to explain his views. Listen patiently and attentively. Don't interrupt him. After he has done speaking, first convey your agreement on whatever points you agree on. If you can't find even a few points of agreement, think hard. Still, if you can't find points of agreement, compromise and agree to some of his points. Remember, you can't always have your way, and that too fully. Stress the points of agreement and keep repeating them. Even if

you think he is absolutely wrong, don't flatly contradict him. Instead, say he is right in his thinking and has reasons to do so. You show that you have an open mind, which will encourage him to keep his mind open, too. Once a background is created this way, the other person will have a proper frame of mind to digest your disagreement. Now, convey your disagreement gently, without anger. Put across your views; soft paddle your opinion. Present your idea in the form of a question rather than a statement. Use phrases like 'How about this?', 'What do you think about this?', or 'What if you were to be on the other side of the table? This way, people will be more willing to listen and less quick to bristle. Hence, never get into an argument. Your aggressiveness will make the other person dig in his heels and stick to his opinion with even more force. Of course, eventually, it is a game of power. Whoever is more powerful will have his way, but the decisions are likely to be accepted without much bitterness if you adopt the above approach. You may win the argument by not listening and dictating your views, but it will strain relationships, and people will retaliate at the first opportunity.

7.6 VALUE CUSTOMER FEEDBACK

- Remove the word complaint from your organisational dictionary. Develop a culture in your organisation that treats customer complaints as customer feedback. This is not just a jumble of terms. Beyond switching terms, it reflects the attitude of your staff and the organisation as a whole. This attitude can make a sea change in how you treat your customers.
- Value customer feedback.
- Take all feedback positively and also respond to it positively, gracefully, and promptly. Of course, responding to adverse feedback about your business is never a comfortable position to be in.
- Customer complaints can be irritating, but keep in mind that someone took the time to write you a letter or email. So you need to respect their time by responding professionally and graciously.
- If the customer complains about your Project Manager, take this seriously. Don't defend it. More often than not, they are right. Don't

make it a prestige issue. Transfer him elsewhere and provide another Project Manager to the customer.

- If you are working in the customer care department, it may be your primary responsibility to attend to customers. However, even if you are not working in the customer care department, you can still get involved in attending to customers, regardless of your department. Such things, however small they may appear, make a lot of difference. Ordinary organisations become great organisations by paying attention to such things. So the better your response to the customers, the better the organisation seems to the customer.

7.7 OPEN AN EMOTIONAL ACCOUNT WITH THE CUSTOMER

Written communication is important, but one thing that scores high in getting the desired results is the relationship with the customer. Though a good relationship by itself doesn't necessarily ensure success, the absence of cordial relationships will make it difficult to achieve the desired results.

Open an emotional account with your customer. Opening an emotional account means reaching a stage in relationships when your customer is able to feel your pain. He appreciates your difficulties. He has empathy for you rather than merely sympathy for you. If you have opened an emotional account with the customer, it will lubricate your relationship. You will have a frictionless, or at least a less-friction relationship. You will be privileged to have the benefit of the doubt, or discretionary decisions are likely to go in your favour. Some smart batsmen keep talking to umpires (instead of their co-batsmen) during the spare time between the two overs. The talk could be very general in nature. For example, "Today it is very hot." Or "Beautiful weather today." They try to develop a relationship with the umpire. Through continuous interactions, they occupy space in the umpire's heart. When such a relationship is developed, the umpire is likely to give the benefit of the doubt to such a batsman on more occasions. Of course, the third umpire has the authority to overrule the on-field umpire's decision in DRS. However, the third umpire can do so only if unambiguous and conclusive evidence is available. If no such evidence is available, he has to uphold the on-field umpire's decision, even if it was apparently the wrong one. Hence, to this extent, it benefits the batsman, who has developed a relationship with the umpire.

If you have opened an emotional account with the customer, he will support you or praise you in front of his superiors. He may try to cover up your minor lapses. If his boss is contemplating some punitive action against you, he may try his best to stall it.

- Deserve and earn empathy.
- Develop and nurture cordial relationships with the customer.
- Cement your relationship.
- Reinforce your bond.
- Dissolve your differences.
- Galvanise the personal touch.
- Build bridges with the customer.

7.8 PRE-SPEAKING WITH THE CUSTOMER

Human beings, in general, do not like surprises. This is a normal human tendency. If all of a sudden a new issue comes up, our response to that issue will be in the form of a knee-jerk reaction. However, if the same issue is not new but has been under discussion for a long time, our response to it will be normal. A survey was conducted to ascertain the agreement or otherwise of the general public on the issue of enacting a law that makes same-sex marriage legally valid. As many as 80% of the respondents responded to this survey with a knee-jerk type of reaction, opining that it is ridiculous to make same-sex marriage legal. The same survey was repeated after one year. During the second survey, only 35% of people disagreed with such an enactment, compared to 80% in the previous survey. What was the reason for such a drastic decline in people opposing such an enactment? This happened because, during the first survey, the issue was new. It had a surprising element. However, during the period between the two surveys, the issue was being discussed in newspapers, television debates, and social media, and hence it was no longer a new issue. The public was now familiar with the issue. This was the main reason for a drastic reduction in the percentage of people opposing such an enactment.

This also applies to international relations between countries. When one country wanted to take a small-scale military action against its neighbouring country, the foreign affairs minister of that country went around the world and pre-informed all important countries that they were likely to take such an action, and thus they were taken into confidence. If no such pre-informing had taken place, all countries would have given a knee-jerk type of reaction condemning this military action upon receiving this news from the media. However, none of the pre-informed countries gave such a knee-jerk reaction, even though other non-pre-informed countries condemned the military action. Thus, pre-informing helped a lot in managing reactions from other countries. Pre-informing or pre-speaking means that you are giving importance to others. It signifies that you are not keeping them in the dark. It means you value the relationship. It means you are taking them into confidence in advance. If you don't pre-speak, the response can be in the form of a knee-jerk reaction. This is because it contains a surprise element. Pre-speaking brings familiarity with the issues. Once you pre-speak, the issue is no longer a new one, so the surprise element disappears. Even if the message is negative, don't hesitate to pre-inform. Pre-informing will at least help to control the damage.

- Pre-speak with the customer before issuing a letter. If you are planning to apply for a revision of rates because of the enlargement of the contract period, informally prepare a background for this and tell your customer in advance that you are going to submit such an application in the coming days for his kind consideration. This will avoid a knee-jerk reaction when he receives such an application. This needs to be done at all levels. This is because, in all organisations, barring proprietary organisations, decisions are taken by a group of officers rather than a single individual, bringing group dynamics into play. For a favourable decision, you need blessings from everyone in the hierarchy. Even if one person is against you, a favourable decision becomes difficult.
- In addition to informing the customer in advance, some of the important letters may require showing the draft to the customer. This is a good practice. Don't send the draft by post or e-mail. Meet him personally with the draft printed in double space. Write 'Draft for kind

review' on top in bold letters and also on each page in a watermark. Accept unharmful suggestions gracefully. Don't defend what you have written merely for the sake of defending. Don't argue unnecessarily. Once you show the draft of any letter to your customer and he corrects it, it becomes his letter. He will defend you when the letter reaches his superiors in his organisation. He will become your ambassador. Of course, when you present the draft to the customer, you run the risk of the customer making unacceptable suggestions. This risk is worth taking. The advantages of showing the draft to customers far outweigh the potential risks. Even if such a situation arises, you can always come out of it tactfully. To counter such situations, you have two escape routes at your disposal. Suppose the suggestion given by the customer is really harmful to your organisation. In that case, you can always take shelter under the umbrella of your company policy and politely bring this policy to his attention. Alternatively, you can say that the final vetting is done by your corporate office or your boss.

- Pre-speaking is also required before an important meeting. Before a formal meeting, speak individually with all participants and advocate for or lobby for your views. By pre-speaking, you nurture their egos and avoid possible knee-jerk types of untoward reactions during the meeting.

7.9 DEPERSONALISATION

- Delink issues from personalities.
- Focus on the subject and not on the object.
- Dissolve your ego while dealing with the customer.
- Don't attack anyone personally, and never in public. Maintain a professional tone. It is possible to make your position clear without attacking anyone personally.
- If you attack someone personally, and that too in public, he will have no option but to activate his defence mechanism. Hence, don't force a situation wherein the other person will have to activate his defence mechanism. He will forget all the good you might have done for him.
- Provide an opportunity to facilitate a graceful exit.

- When there is a dispute, both parties get worked up. They shift their attention from the subject of the dispute (the matter in dispute) to the object of the dispute (the other party). You start generalising the behaviour of the other party and start hating him as a person. You start thinking about what he has done to you and others in the past. When you are so worked up against him as a person, dispute resolution becomes rather impossible.

7.10 ESCALATION OF ISSUES

Sometimes, you may have to escalate the matter to a higher level if the person to whom you have addressed your request is not responding despite follow-up and reminders. However, don't do this discreetly. Do this after creating a sufficient background and only after consulting him and getting his informal permission to escalate the matter. Even if he doesn't give permission, it is fine. You are quite safe, as you have approached him for permission, and hence it will not surprise him.

During the entire process of escalation, keep the lower officer fully involved. After all, he is your normal point of contact. You only approach the higher officers in exceptional circumstances. If you are writing to a higher officer, endorse the copy to the lower officer. If you want to have a meeting with the higher officer, request the lower officer to help you get an appointment. Immediately after the meeting with the higher officer, meet the lower officer and report the developments.

7.11 MEDIATION

If differences or disputes have remained unresolved for a long time and reaching an amicable resolution appears difficult, consider involving a mediator. A mediator can solve the dispute because he focuses on the subject of the dispute and delinks it from personalities. Whereas your thinking is crowded by prejudices, biases, or emotions, the mediator has no such old baggage and hence he can think rationally, purely based on the merits of the case. Also, while both parties have a financial stake in the matter of dispute, the mediator has no such stake. Moreover, the customer is more likely to accept the mediator's decision. If the customer accepts the mediator's decision, you are a winner on two counts. Firstly, you are able to get a favourable resolution of your differences or disputes, which was otherwise not possible through self-effort. Secondly, you can continue to maintain a cordial relationship with the customer.

7.12 THE DILEMMA: TO WRITE OR NOT

As regards correspondence with the customers, the contractors are always in a dilemma about whether to write or not. On one hand, there is a requirement to maintain contemporary records to document the delays or defaults on the part of the customer. On the other hand, they always apprehend that such correspondence may antagonise the customer, and the customer may react violently. For a contractor, it is absolutely necessary to have continued cooperation from the customer throughout the execution of the project. This is because the Engineer-in-charge has many discretionary powers. No contractor can function without active cooperation from the customer. Hence, many times the contractors prefer to refrain from indulging in unpleasant correspondence with the customer.

However, we must always remember that contemporary records are absolutely necessary when it comes to adjudicating differences or disputes at a later date. Fearing a violent reaction, if you are not recording the delays as and when they occur, you run the risk of your genuine claims getting rejected in the absence of contemporary records. So the contractor needs to take a considered call. He needs to weigh all the pros and cons. Usually, the advantages of maintaining contemporary records and correspondence with the customer far outweigh their disadvantages. Even if there is a possibility that such contemporary correspondence may antagonise the customer, it is necessary to maintain such records. Also, an officer may get transferred, and a new officer may take over the charge. In such cases, it is all the more important that the events that took place at the site are well documented. A new incumbent has no way to ascertain past happenings except through records. Thus, from whichever angle you look at it, maintaining records is justified, and there is no reason to avoid writing letters, fearing an unpleasant reaction from the customer.

Is there any via media? Can you not write tactfully without offending the customer? Could you not record the delay without hurting the customer? Yes, if we write tactfully, it is possible to record all types of delays without hurting the customer. We need not blame the customer or accuse him. We may just record the facts and delays without becoming a judge as to who is responsible for the delay. Many times, the delays that are taking place are even beyond the control of the customer. The customer may be trying his best to resolve the issues, but many times he may be helpless as other authorities may not be taking the necessary actions to resolve the issues. In such cases, you can write: "We wish to bring to your kind notice that the encroachment at … km remains unresolved for… months. We appreciate your efforts in arranging a meeting with the District Administration, who promised to look into the matter. However, despite your and our continued follow-up in the last… months, the encroachment still exists." This way, you are not only acknowledging the efforts of the customer in resolving the issues, but at the same time, the delay is also getting recorded without hurting the customer. The customer would not mind such records. Even if a copy of such a letter is endorsed to a higher-level officer, it is fine, as you are acknowledging the efforts of the Engineer-in-charge in resolving the issues. The Engineer-in-charge will not apprehend that his boss will apportion the blame to him. Similarly, for example, if traffic diversion permission is not granted to you because of an ensuing festival like Ganpati Visarjan, you can record this delay, highlighting the festival. The customer would not mind recording such delays, as they are beyond his control, and there is no possibility of anyone blaming him for them. Hence, let the fear not dictate your decision to write or not. Let merit dictate this.

Another solution is that you may ask your Head Office to issue such letters where you expect an unpleasant reaction from the customer. This way, as a Project Manager at the site, you continue to maintain cordial relationships with the customer.

8

THE REAL-LIFE EXAMPLES OF BUSINESS WRITING

*P*resenting below a manual of real-life examples of business writing, demonstrating all the aspects of good business writing, including strategy, structure, composition, tone, selection of words and phrases, punctuation, formalities, etc.:

8.1 SITUATION-BASED BUSINESS WRITING

Sr.	Example
1	**Prompting a response**
	If a creditor wants to drag his debtor to court for non-payment of his dues, it is necessary to establish that these dues are undisputed. One can't drag a debtor to court for non-payment of dues if the dues are disputed. In such cases, the disputes are to be resolved first, and the debt should become undisputedly payable. Only thereafter can he begin the recovery proceedings.
	In such situations, the lawyers deploy a technique that is quite popular among lawyers. They write to the debtor:
	"You owe 75,250$ to my client, Mr. ... Every time my client approached you for payment, you have been promising that payment would be released to him shortly. However, despite your repeated promises over the last two years, you have not released the payment to my client.

I hereby give you a notice of thirty days to release the above overdue outstanding payment of 75,250$ to my client, failing which I will have no option but to initiate appropriate legal proceedings against you on behalf of my client."

The debtor, who had not bothered to reply to any of the routine letters or reminders from the creditor in the last two years, replied per return post:

"We are surprised to receive your letter. The outstanding amount stated by you is absolutely incorrect. We owe only Rs. 32,500$ to your client and not Rs. 75,250$ as wrongly stated by you."

The strategy of the lawyer to provoke the debtor worked beautifully well. Now that the debtor himself has acknowledged that he owes 32,500$, it is easy for the creditor to drag him to a court of law for non-payment.

| 2 | **Prompting a response** |

We paid a 20% advance to one vendor when we placed an order for one piece of equipment. Subsequently, the order was cancelled as he lengthened his delivery period. Despite rigorous follow-up, several reminders in writing and phone calls, he didn't refund the advance or even bothered to reply to the letters. Eventually, we wrote,

"Reaching your office at 11 a.m. on October 25th to collect the refund of the advance."

We got a response.

"I'm out of the office on the 25th." You may come on the 26th."

| 3 | **Avoiding an ill-conceived strategy** |

We lodged a complaint with the publisher about the poor quality of the printing. We repeatedly reminded them, but received no response. In the next reminder, we wrote: "Have you forwarded our complaint to the printer?"

We received a reply the same day stating, "We have already forwarded your complaint to the printer. We will get back to you as soon as we receive a response from the printer."

An ill-conceived strategy made it easy for him to reply, and he instantly grabbed this opportunity. We need to avoid questions that are easy to reply to.

In order to repair the damage, we had to adopt a new strategy. We wrote, "We need 250 copies of the book. Please send your offer for this bulk order. We are confident that you will address our earlier comments when you supply this lot.

We received a reply per return mail: "We are pleased to attach our offer for the supply of 250 copies. Our printer has made the necessary modifications to his machine and confirmed that the next lot will not have any quality-related issues."

| 4 | **Applying for a job** |

Dear Sir,

I am writing to express my interest in the Graphic Designer position at your company. I was excited to see this job posting on the careers page of your company's website. I believe I'd be a great fit for the role.

I am pleased to enclose my resume for your kind perusal. Apart from my educational qualifications and prior experience, the resume also details some of my exemplary accomplishments in design.

After completing a basic graduation course in Graphics at … University, I took several courses to enhance my design skills and overall aesthetic. Since graduating, I've held roles as a Graphic Designer where I've been able to use my in-depth knowledge of colour theory, font pairings, and design software to create visually appealing logos, brochures, flyers, and more. I believe your company would greatly benefit from my experience and animation abilities.

I would love to arrange an opportunity for us to discuss the role further. I look forward to hearing from you and learning more about this exciting opportunity.

Thanking you,

Sincerely,

| 5 | **Pitching for a retainer ship as an accounting firm** |

Dear Sir,

I understand from our mutual acquaintance, Mr… that you are looking to retain an accounting firm to assist you in the sale of your business. I wish to offer my services to you for the above task. I would welcome the opportunity to show you how our firm could help Mr… successfully sell his business earlier this year.

As you'll see on our website, my associates and I have extensive experience in financial accounting, internal audits, tax compliance, and mergers and acquisitions. For the past several years, we have specialised in business evaluation and transition services for sellers. We enjoy working closely with clients throughout the sale process to ensure a smooth transition. As our clients can attest, our various pre-sale price improvement strategies can significantly optimise a business's sale price.

If you're thinking of buying another business, please keep in mind that we also provide business acquisition services. For your convenience, I have enclosed additional information describing the full range of services we provide to our esteemed customers.

We shall be pleased to meet your good self at your kind convenience to discuss your specific needs.

Best Regards.

6	**Situation: Invitation to attend a conference** Dear Mr. ..., I am the President of the Federation of Contractors. We are holding a conference on ..., at the Federation's Head Quarter at ... I am pleased to invite you to this prestigious event. May I also request your good self to give a speech and grace this event with your esteemed expertise? I believe you'd be a great fit for our line-up of speakers, given your distinguished background in the construction industry. A line of reply confirming your presence will help us make the proper arrangements. I look forward to speaking with you. Thanking you, Sincerely,
7	**Situation: An internal note requesting approval for software procurement** You are in charge of one of your company's most important divisions, and your division urgently needs new software. You are writing an internal note to your boss asking for approval of your proposal. The first step is to scribble points that you may like to include in your note to your boss. To start with, these points can be in random order, activating a Madman character in your thought process. The list of points that you need to cover may include: • Preamble • Current software available with your division • The list of state-of-the-art software available in the market • The list of software shortlisted by you • The final negotiated commercial proposal for the purchase of software • Advantages of the proposed software

- Online and offline manuals from the vendor
- Post-installation support from the vendor, including the training of staff in your division
- Proposed lifespan of the software
- The new business that you may acquire post-installation of the software

Preparation of such a list will save a lot of time when you wear the hat of an Architect and start arranging these topics in logical order. For a better presentation, you may like to categorise these points under a few main categories. Having identified the main headings, you may now place the initial points from your random list in the proper category and in a logical sequence. Now you are in a much better position to start writing the note.

Dear Sir,

Sub: Request for approval for software procurement

1. Preamble

The existing software available with our division was procured five years ago. In the last five years, lots of developments have taken place in this field, and several new versions of this category of software have come into the market. Most of our competitors possess state-of-the-art software. We are unable to compete with them in the absence of software that matches the software available to them. It is rather now urgent to procure the latest software and upgrade our capabilities.

2. Overall market scenario for the software

With the development of integrated software in the market, hitherto existing traditional types of software have become outdated. The new state-of-the-art software is capable of providing total business solutions under one platform. These software are user-friendly, highly effective, and cost-efficient.

3. Procurement proposal

3.1 Vendor short-listing process

There are seven vendors for this type of software. Each vendor has specific types of customers to whom they cater. We shortlisted three vendors and had extensive discussions with them.

3.2 Proposed Vendor

After thoroughly examining the shortlisted proposals, we are finally zeroing in on ABC software.

3.3 Cost of procurement

The total all-inclusive cost of this software is …$, including taxes.

3.4 Post-installation support

This cost includes training for our staff and one year's post-installation support from the vendor. The vendor will provide extensive post-installation training for our staff. This training will be both classroom and practical. We have identified a team of six people from our division who will undergo this training from the vendor. The vendor has also agreed to update the version as and when a new version comes up. The vendor will do this for the next three years.

3.5 Financing

This being a capital purchase, funds will be arranged from the Corporate Office as per our normal practice. We have kept the Corporate Finance Department informed throughout the proposal stage about the necessary funds and their schedule.

	4. New business opportunities Post installation and commissioning of this software, we will be able to secure new orders, which we are currently unable to secure. It is expected that the installation of this software will add …$ to the top line and …$ to the bottom line, giving an attractive pay-back period of three years. The proposal is submitted for your kind approval. Thanking you, (You will observe that by scribbling the points, even if they were in random order, you could crystalise your thoughts. This helped a lot in preparing the final version of the note much faster. Now you can do the final editing of this note. You may wear a hat of approving authority and read it as if your staff has submitted this proposal to you for your approval. Consider the questions that will come to your mind or your boss's mind as approving authority. If you can think of some points that may arise in your boss's mind as approving authority, try to proactively answer these points in the note in the first place. This will help in speedy approval of your proposal without back-and-forth correspondence.)
8	**Situation: Pre-tender exclusivity agreement for civil works in Electric Substation** You are a local civil contractor. A foreign MNC is keen to take on Electric Substation projects in your country. However, they are interested only in supplying their equipment. They don't want to get involved in civil works. On the other hand, the Government wants a total solution, including civil works. So the MNC gives civil works to you on a back-to-back basis. Whenever there is a tender inquiry for an Electric Substation, the first thing they do is obtain a quotation for civil works from you.

It was observed that they awarded only one project to you last year, though quotations were given for twenty projects. This poor conversion rate is worrisome for you, as you spend a lot of time preparing quotations. The foreign company finally submitted their tenders for only seven projects, though they obtained quotations from you for twenty projects. This means that the foreign company was obtaining quotations from you even if they were not serious about participating in the project. Also, out of the seven projects they attempted, they succeeded in only three projects but awarded only one project to you. This means that the foreign company was awarding work to someone else despite your helping them at the pre-tender stage.

You need a solution for this situation. After lots of brainstorming, it was decided to charge a nominal fee of 25,000$ for the preparation of a quotation. However, if this quotation gets converted into an order, the above fee of 25,000$ will be refunded by way of credit from the bills when raised. This understanding was formally recorded through a Pre-tender Exclusivity Agreement as follows;

PRE-TENDER EXCLUSIVITY AGREEMENT

PROJECT :

This Exclusivity Agreement of mutual understanding is signed at ….. on the ……… between M/s … having its local registered office at …, (hereinafter referred to as the **First Party**) on one part and M/s … having its registered office at …, (hereinafter referred to as the **Second Party**) on the other part.

WITNESSETH

Whereas the **First Party** has decided to proceed with the bidding of the above project.

And whereas **First Party** approached **Second Party** to submit its best competitive offer to them for the civil works involved in the aforesaid Project.

Whereas the **Second Party** has represented and convinced the **First Party** that it has in its possession the requisite and relevant qualifications, expertise, experience, credentials, and personnel to carry out the civil works for which all necessary approvals from the Customer will be arranged by the **First Party**.

Whereas the **Second Party** has intended to execute Civil works of the above Project on an exclusive basis if the **First Party** succeeds in the said bid.

Now, therefore, in consideration of the premises and of the covenants and conditions set forth, both parties agree hereto as follows:

ARTICLE 1

The **First Party** shall deposit an amount of 25,000$ with the **Second Party** to cover the cost of tender preparation by the **Second Party.**

ARTICLE 2

Upon being successful in getting awarded the above project, the **First Party** will automatically award Civil works to the **Second Party** in which case the amount of 25,000$ deposited as per Article 1 above may be refunded to the **First Party** by way of adjusting the same from the payment to be made to **Second Party**

ARTICLE 3

And whereas both parties have undertaken and agreed that, subsequent to the signing of this agreement, they shall not make any offer or deal with any other party, the **First Party** hereby binds to award the execution of Civil works to the **Second Party** for the aforesaid Project.

	ARTICLE 4 A separate agreement will be prepared subsequently to cover the detailed terms and conditions of this agreement. **ARTICLE 5** This agreement is valid for 180 days from the date of signing. ------------------------------- **FIRST PARTY** **SECOND PARTY** (This strategy worked very well. This agreement reduced the number of quotation requests from twenty per year to three, of which two resulted in orders.)
9	**Situation: Non-payment of bills** Your bills have not been paid for over six months by your customer, –a Government organisation. This is despite the provision in the contract that stipulates payment within thirty days and payment of interest if it remains unpaid even after a grace period of an additional thirty days. You have decided to write to your customer. You have to ask yourself what you want to accomplish through this communication. The answer to this question will determine what you write and the tone you use.

Scenario 1: The purpose is to focus on the release of payments.

Tone: Friendly and extending cooperation with a solution-arriving approach

Dear Sir,

Project:

Subject: Request for prioritising the release of outstanding payments

As you are aware, the above project is progressing quite well and as per the schedule stipulated by your good self. We wish to bring to your kind attention our concern about delays in the release of payments for this Project.

We request you to kindly see if it is possible to give a little more priority in releasing payment for this prestigious project. We have all the resources available with us at the site. If the payment flow continues uninterruptedly, we will be able to complete the project on schedule even now, despite the unfortunate delay that has taken place in the release of payment so far.

We are aware that several projects are going on in this region under your able stewardship, and the budget allocated by the Government is limited. Appreciating this difficulty, we are even prepared to forego the payment of interest, which is payable as per the terms of the contract. We believe this gesture of ours will certainly help you get more funds allocated for this project.

We suggest we meet at your kind convenience and discuss this proposal to arrive at a solution. In our opinion, it would be advisable if the representative from the Finance Department also attends this meeting.

Looking forward to meeting you soon.

Thanking you, and assuring you of our best attention always,

Scenario 2: The purpose is to serve notice for interest payments.

Tone: Urgency and insisting on contractual rights

Dear Sir,

Project:

Subject: Request for immediate release of overdue outstanding payments, together with interest.

We wish to bring to your kind attention our growing concern about continued inordinate delays in the release of payments for this Project.

The details of outstanding bills, dates of their submission, due dates of payment as per the terms of the contract, no. of days for which payment is overdue, and interest payable are tabulated in the enclosed Annexure I. The interest payable has been worked out as per clause no. … of the contract.

We request you release the above outstanding payments, together with interest, immediately, without further delay.

Thanking you, and assuring you of our best attention always,

Scenario 3: The purpose is to serve notice for termination.

Tone: Firm but without burning bridges

Dear Sir,

Project:

Subject: Notice of Termination

As you are aware, payments for this project have been delayed inordinately ever since the inception of the project. We have been bringing this to your attention from time to time.

Both the magnitude of the outstanding payment and the age of remaining overdue are unprecedented. This default on your part has caused a material adverse effect on the project's cash flow and its viability. In addition, the land acquisition progress continues to remain extremely poor.

Under the circumstances, we hereby serve this notice of termination in terms of clause no. ... of the contract.
We will be pleased to associate with you in the future if there is a suitable opportunity.

Thanking you, and assuring you of our best attention always,

(This simple example shows how the tone of the letter and choice of words and phrases change with a change in the purpose of the letter, even when the underlying situation is the same.)

10 Situation: Misunderstanding about imported content in a BOQ item

Dear Sir,

PROJECT :

REF: Your Letter No... Dt...

We acknowledge with thanks the receipt of the above-referred letter and wish to submit as follows:

1) The observation regarding item No.1 of the Performa Invoice is probably because of a misunderstanding in reading, translating, and interpreting the description of this item out of context without taking into consideration the full background of the issue.

    As you are aware, each imported item is required to be linked with the corresponding BOQ item. This is a requirement of the Finance Department. Accordingly, LCs are opened in line with BOQ items. Also, as per normal established practice, the item description in LC is kept the same as the BOQ item description. Once LC is opened using the item description given in the BOQ, all other documents, like packing list, invoice, etc., also have to be necessarily in line with the description written in LC.

Thus, the reading, translation, and interpretation of this item need to be done keeping in view the above background.

2) Item 1 of Invoice No. ... corresponds to and borrows its description from item No. 14 of Power System BOQ, which is a parent source document that reads:

"Provide and lay in protective PVC Pipe, connect and test Low Voltage Cable NYY ... Sq.mm., according to drawing No. ... complete and tested as specified"

Here, the imported portion of this BOQ item is only cables and PVC pipes are locally arranged and installed at the site. The above misunderstanding has arisen because of the requirement that the description in LC must be the same as the BOQ item description.

3) When no pipes or conduits are required and cables are laid bare, the BOQ item description rightly eliminates PVC pipes e.g. Item 2 of the invoice, which corresponds to item 15 of BOQ of Power System, which reads:

"Supply of ... Kv Cable XLPE ... Sq.mm. including all necessary sleeves, sealing ends according to drawing No. ... complete and tested as specified."

Accordingly, for this item, the invoice does not mention PVC pipes and rightly so.

Trust the above explanation of the context and background of the issue, clarifies the above misunderstanding.

Best regards.

11	**Situation: The contractor's refusal to rectify defects during DLP**

Dear Sir,

Sub: Contractual obligation to rectify the defects during the Defect Liability Period

Ref.:

We are rather surprised to receive your letter dated...

As a part of DLP contractual requirements, a joint inspection of the developed footpath and installed facilities from ... to ... was carried out on ... along with your representative, and a list of snag points prepared jointly was sent to you vide our letter dated ... for rectifications and submission of a compliance report.

However, instead of attending to snag points and submitting a compliance report, you have pointed out extraneous reasons for damages. You have made an attempt to attribute these defects to a variety of causes, such as local accidents, theft by miscreants, damage from works carried out by other agencies, damage from vehicles plying and parked on the footpath, and so on. You have also mentioned that you have already submitted 'As built' drawings and concluded yourself that the process of handing over the developed footpath and facilities to the Employer stand completed.

As you are aware, the Contract has a provision for DLP for two years. The developed footpath and installed facilities are obviously for the benefit of the public and commuters. All construction-related defects and damages, when found under usage, have to be attended to and corrected to their original status over the DLP. The fact that these footpaths are opened to the public for use in no way dilutes the contractor's liability to maintain them in good working conditions during DLP. Be informed that you can't be absolved from your contractual obligations during the DLP on the ground that footpaths are being used by the public. Also, please note that 'As built' drawings submitted by you are meant to serve

	as documentation for recording the work actually executed on site and have nothing to do with DLP obligations to rectify defects.

During the next quarterly joint inspection, we shall review this snag list and add further defects, if any. In the meantime, you are once again notified to rectify these defects on priority and provide us with a compliance report.

Thanking You,

(The letter strongly repudiates the contractor's attempt to escape DLP obligations. It gives a cogent argument and logical reasons to justify the Employer's stand. The message is conveyed emphatically in no uncertain terms and in a polite yet firm tone.) |
| 12 | **Situation: A customer complaint threatening contract termination**

Purpose: To extinguish the fire and avert the crisis

Tone: Extremely submissive and apologetic

Dear Sir,

We acknowledge with thanks the receipt of your letter dated … We appreciate your valued feedback. We, from the Corporate Office, have taken serious note of the lapses pointed out by your good self. We have initiated a series of corrective actions.

As regards points 1) to 3) of your letter, we wish to submit the following:
1) We regret the inconvenience caused due to inadequate appreciation of site conditions on our part. Based on a proper appreciation of site conditions, we have now redesigned the structure, and the revised design has since been discussed with your good self and submitted for your kind review. |

2) We note your instructions given during the site visit of ... regarding changes to be made in the structure. We were to submit the revised drawings on the day of the site visit by 6:00 p.m. We very much regret the delay in submitting the revised drawings as per your requirement, which have since been submitted on ...
3) We wish to submit that, because of unavoidable circumstances, Mr. ..., our Team Leader could not be present during the site visit of Friday. We wish to state that Mr. ... has since left the organisation and in his place, Mr. ... has taken charge.

We once again regret the inconvenience caused and wish to assure you, Sir, that we shall leave no stone unturned in fulfilling our obligations to you under the contract and that we shall diligently satisfy all your requirements in time.

Thanking you, and assuring you our best attention always,

(You will observe from the draft that the complaint from the customer has been treated as valued feedback. Following the BLU strategy, the reply upfront states that the corporate office has taken a series of corrective actions based on this feedback. The tone of the letter has the power to extinguish the fire.
Do not hesitate to reply in a submissive and apologetic tone, if the same can extinguish the fire.)

8.2 UNDESIRABLE AND DESIRABLE VERSIONS

Presented below are a few examples of undesirable and desirable versions in business writing, with commentary explaining the critical differences between the two versions:

Sr.	Example
1	**Don't make general statements.**
	Undesirable version:
	Mr. X's performance as CEO of the company is not good. (This is merely a general statement. It may give the impression that this is only a personal opinion of the writer, as he has given no reason in support of his statement.)
	Desirable version:
	Mr. X's performance as CEO of the company is unsatisfactory. During his tenure as CEO, Mr. X inorganically expanded the business by acquiring unrelated companies. These acquisitions increased the debt by ... million $. It was expected that profits from these newly acquired companies would be used to repay this debt and bring it to zero in five years. However, this has not been achieved.
	(This is a specific statement as opposed to the general statement in the previous version. Provide your readers with concrete information. Don't try to push them with an abstract.)

| 2 | **Give reasons for rejecting a proposal.** |

Undesirable version:

The proposal, advocating for the purchase of aggregate rather than self-manufacturing, merits rejection. Accepting this proposal will not be beneficial for the company.

(This version assumes familiarity. It takes for granted that the reader himself will be able to ascertain the reasons for rejection. The matter in this version will invite counter questions involving time-consuming back-and-forth correspondence.)

Desirable version:

I am unable to agree with the proposal, which advocates buying aggregate instead of self-manufacturing it. The reasons are as follows:

1) The proposal is likely to create a monopoly situation, leading to the company being blackmailed by a handful of vendors.
2) It has been assumed that the aggregate price will remain constant over the next two years. This assumption appears to be invalid.
3) The proposal highlights the required capital cost and rejects the self-manufacturing proposal on the grounds of capital cost alone. However, this is based on invalid perceptions of the facts. The proposal of self-manufacturing has a payback period of two years, i.e. it will pay back its capital costs in two years. This is because self-manufactured aggregates are 20% cheaper.

(This version logically presents a viewpoint and convinces the reader about the proposal.
Note the credibility that this version provides through specific reasoning.)

3	**Give reasons for rejecting a proposal.**
	Undesirable version:
	I am rejecting Mr. X's proposal, which assumes a constant interest rate scenario over the next five years.
	(The writer has not given any convincing reason for rejecting the proposal nor offered an alternative solution. Also, the arrogance of the writer is clearly visible. The tone of rejection is likely to hurt the proposer's self-esteem, and if the proposer is also equally egoistic, this may result in personality conflict, leading to a long chain of avoidable letter exchanges. The focus is likely to shift away from the proposal and the solution.)
	Desirable version:
	Mr. X has submitted a detailed and well-presented proposal. The viability of this proposal hinges on our estimate of future interest rates. As we know, the Central Bank announces monetary policy on a bimonthly basis. While estimating a five-year interest rate scenario is extremely difficult, we can safely make an educated guess of the probable interest rate scenario over a two-year time horizon. Accordingly, I believe a two-year horizon is the optimum period for correctly evaluating this proposal. I humbly suggest reworking the proposal and duly restricting the horizon to two years.
	(The writer has not only given convincing reasons for rejecting the proposal but also offered an alternative solution. He has also soft-paddled his rejection, making it palatable. The humility of the writer is clearly visible. Unlike the previous version, the proposer is more likely to digest this rejection.)

4 | **Undesirable version:**

Dear Sir,

We regret to inform you that we can't supply 500 copies of the book **'The Art of Negotiation'** at the 60% discount that you asked for. Your demand for a 60% discount is highly unjust. No one, not even best-selling authors, or even the biggest book-selling chains, has ever received such a hefty discount of 60%.

If you'd care to resubmit your request with a more modest figure of 30% discount, we may consider the same at that time, though I can't give you any guarantee.

Desirable version:

Dear Sir,

We are extremely delighted to note that you've decided to distribute 500 copies of our best-selling book **'The Art of Negotiation'** during your prestigious business summit. Congratulations to you on selecting this book. You have chosen the best book available on the subject. We would be delighted to supply 500 copies to you as per your schedule.

We note your desire for a 60% discount. You are justified in demanding the same in view of the large quantity. Our corporate policy applies a 30% discount if the order quantity exceeds 1000. I presented your demand for a 60% discount to top management, and upon perusal, they have approved a 30% discount for 500 copies being ordered by you. Additionally, we shall deliver these copies to your office personally so that delays in couriers, etc. are avoided.

Thanking you, and assuring you of our best attention always,

(Notice the remarkable differences between the two versions. The tone of the first version is highly aggressive.

We should never respond to customers in such an aggressive manner.

	Although the second version offers the same 30% discount as the first version, the tone is extremely soft and palatable. It also proves legitimacy by explaining the corporate policy, which doesn't permit more than a 30% discount.)
5	**Undesirable Version** Dear Sir, **PROJECT: Work of ... awarded to you vide Work Order no.** **SUB: Your request for the release of payment** **REF: Your email dated ...** We are surprised to receive your reminder email related to the payment of the ongoing assignment under Work Order no. ... We would like to state that there is no delay in payment from our side. On the contrary, there are several defaults on your part. Before we consider your bills, we'd like to bring to your attention the following points: 1. Issues with the execution of the work We have been constantly pointing out various issues regarding your poor work execution. The emails also outline the potential financial penalties for you if you delay project execution. 2. Incomplete and improper data submission There are chronic issues regarding the incomplete, inaccurate, and improper data that has been submitted to us that too after prolonged delays, regarding which multiple emails were sent by us. Every time the data has been shared with us, it has been delayed, incomplete and inaccurate. We have never received the complete data with the specified accuracy that needs to be delivered as per the Work Order. We request you follow all the requirements mentioned in the Work Order and submit deliverables in acceptable forms.

Once we receive the data, it will be duly checked by our team for its correctness, accuracy, and completeness. If found correct, the same will be further passed on to the Principal Customer for their comments and acceptance. Upon approval by the Principal Customer, we shall discuss further courses of action based on the Work Order conditions.

Thanking you,

Desirable Version

Dear Sir,

PROJECT: Work of ... awarded to you vide Work Order no.

SUB: Inordinate delay in submission of accurate data complete in all respects as specified in the Work Order

REF: Our email dated ...

The above Work was awarded to you on -----------. Yours being a reputed firm, we expect that you will carry out the work with due diligence as per the best industry practice and in a time efficient manner. However, we observe that there are several issues as regards the work being executed by you. We have been bringing these issues to your notice from time to time. However, despite several reminders, these issues have remained unattended and no corrective actions have been taken by you. Our Principal Customer is extremely unhappy because of the inordinate delay on your part in submitting the required data. We are once again bringing these issues to your notice in a consolidated manner as follows:

1. Issues with the execution of the work

The issues we have been facing regarding the execution of the work done by you have been brought to your notice through various emails sent by us. These emails are listed above. The emails also mention the financial consequences associated with delaying project execution that can be imposed on you.

2. Incomplete and improper data submission

There are multiple issues regarding the data that has been submitted to us that too after inordinate delays, regarding which several emails were sent to you. Every time the data has been shared with us, it has been delayed inordinately apart from being incomplete and inaccurate. We have never received the data with the desired accuracy that needs to be delivered as per the Work Order.

We request you follow all the stipulations mentioned in the Work Order and submit deliverables in acceptable forms.

Once we receive the data from you in acceptable form, this data will be duly checked by our team for its correctness, accuracy, and completeness. If found in order, the same will be passed on to the Principal Customer for their comments and acceptance.

We are rather perturbed to note that instead of taking action to submit accurate data as per the requirements specified in the Work Order, you are unjustifiably talking about the release of payment. You will agree that the question of payment doesn't arise unless accurate and complete data is submitted as specified in the Work Order. The payment will be released as per the terms of the Work Order once you submit accurate and complete data in an acceptable form and the Principal Customer accepts the data.

Thanking you,

(Notice the remarkable differences between the two versions, starting with the framing of the subject of the letter. The first version is characterised by a guilty tone for having delayed the release of payments. It also makes an unsuccessful attempt to justify non-payment by indulging in allegations rather than logically putting forth a convincing argument. The second version is characterised by an aggressive tone focusing on non-performance by the vendor without any guilt. While it highlights non-performance firmly and in clear terms, it also assures the release of payment upon compliance with the terms of the Work Order.)

6	**Undesirable version:**

To

The Project Director,

Dear Sir,

Project:

Subject:

As discussed and agreed during our meeting held on …, we propose to scale down the value of the Performance Bank Guarantee to 1/3 of its original value, i.e. from …$ to …$ and extend the same by six months.

Kindly confirm this is in order. Upon your confirmation, we will approach our bankers to scale down the value of the Bank Guarantee and send you the extension advice, duly scaling down its value to 1/3.
Thanking you,

Desirable version:

To

Dear Sir,

Project:

Subject:

We wish to thank your good self for the kind courtesy extended to the undersigned during the meeting held on …

We have initiated action with our bankers to extend the validity of the Performance Bank Guarantee by six months, scaling down its value to 1/3 of its original value. The extension advice will be sent to you within a week.

Thanking you, |

(Notice the remarkable differences between the two versions. While the first version is highly provocative, the second version is non-provoking. The second version tactfully refrains from making the statement that the Project Director has agreed to scale down the value of the Performance BG. Such a statement will put him in an embarrassing position in his organisation. As per normal organisational practice, for decisions involving BG, the prior consent of the finance department is necessary. The Project Director is not authorised to commit such scaling down, though he may have done so in the interest of the project. The second version tactfully conveys the scaling-down proposal subtly. Whereas the first version provokes them to reply, and that reply will most likely be negative, there is no such provocation to reply in the second version. Most probably, you will not receive any response within a week. Once a period of one-week lapses, you can safely go ahead with scaling down the Bank Guarantee as agreed in the meeting. Later on, the finance department wouldn't be able to object as they had the opportunity to respond but they didn't.)

9

CONTRACTUAL CLAIMS IN THE CONSTRUCTION INDUSTRY

*T*he construction industry is quite different from the manufacturing industry. The construction industry revolves around projects. It has projects with specific durations. One project gets completed at one location, and another project gets started at another location. However, in the manufacturing industry, factories are normally at a fixed location. In the manufacturing industry, a product is manufactured first and then sold. The actual costs are known accurately, making it easy to determine the selling price. However, in the construction industry, a product (like a bridge or dam) is first sold and then constructed. The selling price is pre-decided. It is based on estimates and guesstimations. Additionally, there are numerous variables to consider, such as unexpected subsoil conditions, unexplored underground utilities, changes in product designs or specifications as the project progresses, the time required for statutory permissions and approvals, demands from project-affected individuals, and the impact of adverse climatic conditions. Because of such peculiar characteristics, the probabilities of differences and disputes taking place between the owner and the contractor are quite high in the construction industry as compared to the manufacturing industry.

When differences and disputes arise, the attention of both parties gets diverted, and the progress of the project suffers adversely. It is necessary to resolve such differences and disputes on a priority basis so that the contractor can bring back his focus on the progress of the Project.

9.1 CLAIM LETTER

In the construction industry, resolving differences and disputes takes a long time for a variety of reasons, the primary reason being a poor presentation of the claims by the contractor. Though the quality of presentation improves drastically when it reaches the arbitration stage, initial submissions to the Employer are mostly very casual. The presentation of a claim is an art. Presenting a claim artfully from the outset expedites the resolution of differences and disputes. There are many ways to present the claim. However, the following structured approach may be considered:

1. Introduction

Start with an introduction that gives a brief outline of the submission at the beginning. Picking up the link from this introduction, we can develop the claim later.

2. Preamble to the claim

It is helpful in the beginning to give a resume of any historical data affecting the subject of the claim in as much depth as necessary so that the reader becomes familiar with what you are going to present subsequently. The preamble prepares the reader for what is in store for him.

3. Contractual argument

This is an important part of the presentation. You may start by citing the clause(s) upon which the claim is based and, if required, reproduce the same for ready reference. Based on the provisions of the contract, the cogent and logical argument intended to put the reader in the same mind as the writer should be set out in detail. A cogent argument is one that is capable of being strongly and clearly expressed in a way that influences people's beliefs. It is convincing, sound, and valid. It has a belief-changing power. The reader should buy your message.

4. Citing precedents

Government officers look for precedents. Strengthen their hands by providing a relevant precedent. The precedents that can be considered for citation may include an admission of a similar claim by the same or any other customer, arbitration awards, court judgments, and so on.

5. Conclusion

The concluding paragraph of a claim letter should bring your message to a polite, professional close. It should have an impactful punch that creates a lasting impression on the addressee. It should state what action is required from the addressee. However, you must steer clear of overused or trite phrases to avoid ending your letter poorly.

9.2 FINANCIAL PRESENTATION OF A CLAIM

The financial presentation should be tailor-made to suit particular circumstances and may include derivation of rates, rate analysis, the basis for enhancement of rates, etc. Use the relevant Schedule of Rates published by the Government. While drafting the financial presentation, keep in mind the requirements of the Finance Department of the customer's organisation. Remember, the Finance Department expects that all assumptions made by you, or rates or prices used by you, should be authentic and duly supported by a valid document as per trade practice. Anything that is not supported by a valid document is unlikely to go through.

However, don't be in a hurry to quantify the claim and indicate its total financial implications to the customer early in the claim-building process, especially if the financial implications are quite large. This is because a large-value financial claim tends to create a negative bias in the minds of customers towards the claim from the beginning. So, it would be a good strategy to build up a claim and form the basis for its quantification, but to refrain from actual quantification of total financial implications. Once the customer develops a somewhat affirmative bias towards the claim, you can always quantify it on an already established basis.

In short, the claim letter shall be businesslike, though comprehensive but concise, presenting precise matters of fact without giving anything untoward.

The timing of claims is also important. For example, if the project is running substantially behind schedule, the customer may not entertain your claim. In that case, wait till the project catches up in speed.

9.3 DOCUMENTATION

9.3.1 The importance of documentation in Contract Administration

> *"The horror of that moment," the King went on, "I shall never forget!"*
>
> *"You will, though," the Queen said, "if you don't make a memorandum of it."*
>
> **– Lewis Carroll**

One of the most important aspects of Contract Administration is documentation. Every facet of the construction business requires documentation. The normal average duration of the construction contracts is about three years. After this, a Defect Liability Period of a minimum of one year is involved. Because of the inherent characteristics of the construction industry, many differences and disputes take place during the execution of the project. The resolution of such differences or disputes often takes years or even decades. Thus, the effective life cycle times of construction contracts are quite large. By the time the disputes reach an arbitration tribunal or court, people involved in the project from both sides may not be available. At that time, documents would be the only reliable source to ascertain what exactly happened during the execution of the project.

The supporting documents constitute the most important part of a claim. The acceptance or rejection of a claim that is notified/registered in time and is contractually tenable primarily depends on the strength of the supporting documents. A well-substantiated, robust, and effective document will help in proving the claims, while a disorganised document will make proving the claims difficult and time-consuming. Hence, in anticipation of potential disputes that may probably lead to arbitration, all claims shall be backed up by proper, complete, quantitative, systematic, well-presented, unimpeachable, contemporary, and timely records jointly signed with the customer's authorised representative. Such documentation shall be sound so as to stand the test of legality at a later date in arbitration or court. Usually, it is the responsibility of the Project Manager to ensure such thorough documentation.

In many cases, customers do not readily agree to maintain joint records. In such cases, request the customer persistently, convince them, and seek cooperation. If required, escalate the matter to a higher level. If the customer does not cooperate despite efforts as above, send copies of unilateral records maintained by you (duly summarised systematically) to the customer regularly and promptly by Regd. A. D. post or courier service duly acknowledged and submit a claim based on such records.

9.3.2 Document management and control system

Good documentation on a construction project does not just happen. It requires a careful and concerted effort at all levels of the organisation. It is a consistent application of the 'put it in writing' rule. Documentation consists of the writings, notes, or records of persons who were present at events, contemporaneously written at the time or shortly thereafter. A good document management and control system builds elements, clarifies expectations, establishes official agreements, and protects the interests of both parties.

The extent of record-keeping required for a particular construction job will depend on the type of contract. However, some record keeping will be required in any case because it is:

1) Required by the law
2) Required under the terms of the contract
3) Necessary to control the ongoing work
4) Necessary as supporting data for estimating future work or extra items of work

Each project necessitates a custom-made document management system, depending on the project's complexities.

- Decide which records to maintain and how. Establish logs of the records so that they can be found, referred to, and followed up on as required. This greatly facilitates managing, analysing, and comparing contracts.
- Once the records have been identified, ensure that they are set up, maintained, and used for managing the job.
- Take steps to ensure the accuracy, reliability, and credibility of records. Unreliable records may not be useful in supporting the claim and may even be detrimental.
- Review the record-keeping system from time to time. This is because records have a habit of expanding in unexpected ways. For example, staff down the line may file most of the correspondence in Miscellaneous files rather than appropriate files.
- Records also take up physical and virtual space. Determine the useful life of the different components and take a systematic approach to record disposal.
- A good set of records that might be kept on a typical mid-sized construction project could well include the following files maintained chronologically for ease of retrieval on demand:
- Original Contract Agreement with all constituents and amendments, if any
- Original tender estimate, Construction control budget
- GFC drawings, Shop drawings, including all revisions
- Contract Milestone Schedules, Master Schedules and detailed schedules
- Daily production logs, e.g. concrete pours, RFIs etc.
- Daily equipment use
- Material delivery and utilisation records
- Weekly, monthly, or quarterly progress reports, including time-stamped photographs
- Progress payment billings under the contract
- Accounting records: payroll, accounts payable, and receivable
- Change Notices and Change Orders issued by the owner
- Actual Cost Reports, weekly or monthly, including Exception Reports.

- Contract correspondence, notices of claims for delays and extra costs by the contractor
- Minutes of meetings

9.3.3 Probable list of supporting documents

The supporting documents may include:

- Site records
- Work Diaries
- Instructions and Orders
- Construction Schedules (Bar Charts, CPM/PERT)
- Requests for Inspection (RFIs)
- Daily, Weekly, and Monthly Progress Reports
- Photographs with a time stamp
- Video clippings
- Google images
- Newspaper cuttings
- Charts or Graphical presentation
- Rate Analysis
- Purchase Orders

9.4 INTERNAL CLAIM MANAGEMENT PROCESS

The contractor's internal claim management process needs to be robust enough to ensure a high success ratio in claim realisation. The following tips may help in building such a robust internal process:

- Tender selectively. Don't participate in a cutthroat competition merely to secure a project. Based on a workable price, draw a line and stick to it.
- Develop a Master Schedule (L1) and a Detailed Schedule (L2) for project completion, considering milestones specified in the contract. Also, prepare Resource Schedules for major resources like plant and equipment, materials, manpower, etc. that fit the required dates specified in the contract. Distribute these schedules for information to all concerned, including the Employer and his consultants, so that everyone knows what is expected of them and the schedule thereof, and can plan their inputs effectively.

- Give priority to the timely completion of the project. This goal should be assigned overriding power above all other goals. At the end of the day, the contractor makes more profit if he completes the project on time. This message should be driven home firmly to all people in the organisation.
- Since construction projects are vulnerable to delays by their very nature, allow a cushion of at least 10% of the contract period in your internal programme and accordingly provide more resources so that even if there is a delay to the extent of 10%, the project can still be completed in time.
- Effectively drive home the criticality of time for the Employer, the consultant, the contractor and their sub-contractors.
- Ensure and facilitate that the contractor's main team and their sub-contractors can perform their work without interference or delays by the Employer, consultants, or fellow contractors. As a general contractor, take the lead and coordinate the entire work, including that of the subcontractor, so that project goals are achieved.
- Where close coordination is required, ensure there is proper communication taking place at a level that can have a positive impact on the work.
- Appoint an experienced Document Controller to control the inflow and outflow of documents.
- Maintain the original records in one safe place.
- Inculcate the habit of maintaining records contemporaneously. Even the best of memories are fallible. Hence, contemporary records are a must. After having created records, these records can be extracted, analysed, and presented with a different perspective at any time, but records cannot be fabricated later.
- Photographs are a must for recording purposes. These must show what is actually going on at that time, with the location and viewpoint identified, along with the date and photographer's name. Similarly, you can use authentic videography as supporting evidence for claimable events such as flood or earthquake damages, local agitations by project-affected people, and so forth.

- If the owner or his consultants cause a delay, notify them promptly, politely, and tactfully, but firmly, in writing. Similarly, register and notify all force majeure events promptly.
- Issue the required notices within the time limit stipulated in the contract. The primary goal of the notice is to inform the other party of an event or subject to which it pertains. If you have suffered delays for reasons beyond your control, the notice should describe the event and your intention to claim additional time and money. Similarly, if you intend to stop the work for non-payment, you have to give notice to the customer.
- Periodically, write suitable letters summarising events that have taken place up to the date of the letter. Write tactfully and diplomatically. Avoid the temptation to apportion blame. Control the craving to play the role of a judge yourself. Simply record the facts without assigning blame. Use respectful, professional, and non-hostile language. Avoid derogatory remarks.

9.5 AVOIDING VERBAL INSTRUCTIONS

Insist on written instructions from the Engineer. If the Engineer gives verbal instructions and does not confirm the same in writing, issue a letter to the Engineer within three days confirming the Engineer's verbal instructions.

Important telephonic communication with the Engineer shall also be confirmed in writing within three days.

Insist that instructions are given only by the Engineer and tactfully avoid receiving instructions from an officer other than the Engineer. However, if higher authorities give instructions, get the same confirmed in writing by the Engineer.

9.6 NOTIFYING A CLAIM

The intention to claim an additional payment shall be notified within the time limit specified in the Contract and in definite terms, not vague terms.

For example,

GOOD TYPICAL NOTIFICATION OF A CLAIM

"We acknowledge with thanks the receipt of your instruction vide ..., communicating your requirement to have ... in lieu of ... stipulated in the Contract vide clause number..."

The above variation shall constitute an extra item calling for additional financial compensation.

In pursuance of clause number ----- of the Contract, we hereby notify you of our intention to claim an additional financial compensation."

9.7 REGISTERING A CLAIM

The claim must be registered within the time limit specified in the contract. It must be registered unambiguously.

A GOOD TYPICAL REGISTRATION OF A CLAIM

"We wish to inform you that because of blasting operations at the adjacent site on ... and ..., we had to suspend our site operations three times in a day on both of the above days, resulting in a consequent loss of output and delays in the completion of the project.

In pursuance of clause number ... of the Contract, we hereby register our claim for:

i) Extension of time and
ii) An additional payment

We understand from the contractor at the adjacent site that the blasting operations will continue for a couple of weeks. As soon as the blasting operations conclude, we will promptly submit our claim for:

i) Extension of time and
ii) An additional payment."

9.8 AVOIDING A HALF-HEARTED APPROACH

Be convinced about what you are writing, and write it with passion. Avoid a half-hearted approach. Don't plant seeds of failure in yourself. Avoid weak links in your letter. The customer will pick up the weakest link and dispose of your letter easily. Weak links make the customer's life easy.

Following are some examples that show a half-hearted approach:

- 'We request you to kindly release the outstanding payment of 225,000$ immediately. If this is not possible for any reason, kindly release at least 50,000$.'
- 'We are enclosing the revised GFC drawing, incorporating most of your comments. Trust you will find this in order. If, however, you still insist on incorporating your balance comments, we shall revise the drawing accordingly upon hearing from your good self.'

9.9 GRADUAL BUILD-UP OF A CLAIM FOR PAYMENT OF INTEREST

Delays in the release of payments are quite common in construction projects. Raising claims for interest payments on outstanding dues is always a tricky issue. This should be handled tactfully by gradually building up the claim for payment of interest to avoid violent reactions from the customer.

Step No. 1: "We draw your kind attention to the fact that our three monthly RA Bills are pending for payment. We shall be greatly obliged if these payments are released immediately. This will help us maintain our cash flow and achieve progress as per schedule."

Step No. 2: "The non-release of our outstanding dues is causing a lot of financial strain on us. So far, we have been borrowing funds from our banks at exorbitant interest rates and somehow managing the show, but our banks have now refused to extend any further credit to us."

Step No. 3: "The non-release of our outstanding dues is causing a severe financial strain on us. Our creditors are now restless, and they have stopped or slowed down supplies and services and served us legal notices to clear their dues together with interest."

Step No. 4: "We request you to kindly release the outstanding payment together with the interest."

10

CONCLUSION

*I*n business communication, the quality of the writing is as important as the idea. This is because, based on the quality of your writing, your business associates form an opinion about you, your team, your organisation, and its level of professionalism.

Business writing requires lots of planning, strategising and tactfulness. You need to explain your contention with a logical, cogent, and convincing argument that is powerful enough to change the reader's belief. Your writing should make the reader buy your message.

In addition to the merit of the idea and quality of writing, soft aspects such as pre-speaking with the customers, opening an emotional account with them, developing a transformational relationship with them, etc. are equally important. In fact, getting the desired results through a business letter is a complex issue. A properly strategised, tactfully written, and rightly timed letter, the contractual tenability of your contention, the convincing power of your presentation, the strength of supporting documents, relationships with the customer, relentless follow-up, escalation of the issue if such a need arises, etc., will collectively decide success or otherwise.

By following the strategies, techniques, tools, ideas, and tips provided in the book, you can create a vibrant masterpiece that the reader will love to read and act upon. This is the author's guarantee.

Happy writing!

11

APPENDICES

APPENDIX 1

THE ART OF LISTENING

- The most valuable skill you can possess is listening, as it occupies five minutes out of every ten spent in communication. How well you listen greatly impacts both your personal and professional lives, as well as the quality of your relationships. However, in our fast-paced, ego-centric world, we are often too self-centered to spare our precious time to listen to others, even those we love the most.
- Learn to listen with curiosity, speak with candour, and act with integrity. Listening with curiosity allows relationships to thrive. Telling your truth will enable people to be honest with themselves and with you, and acting with integrity keeps relationships at a high standard. Also, when you lend your ears to others, people enjoy your company even more.
- Learn, cultivate, and master the art of active listening. Whereas hearing is a physiological process that our body innately does, listening is an active process that we must consciously accomplish by making special efforts. Work on all four elements of listening: hearing, interpretation, evaluation, and response. Since the brain can think four times faster than a person can speak, use this gap to evaluate.
- Listening is a process that operates at multiple levels. Listening with the ears is the first step in the process of listening. Listening from the mind is one level of understanding. Listening from your heart with feelings, emotions, and devotion is another level of understanding. Listening

from the very core of your being, or the deepest part of your being, is yet another level of understanding. So don't merely listen with your ears. Listen from the mind. Listen from the heart with feelings, and don't even stop there; get into being. Uplift the level of your listening. The phrase 'I hear what you say' indicates low-level listening.

- Open up your senses and listen earnestly. Listen attentively, keeping your eyes peeled, your ears open, and your mouth shut. Listen silently. The words 'listen' and 'silent' use the same five letters. Listen with a laser-like focus when someone is talking. Don't work or look somewhere else when someone is talking to you. Make the speaker feel that you are listening to him attentively. Discipline yourself to use attentive listening techniques. Attentive listening means hearing what is said as well as comprehending and understanding what is being omitted. Listen by giving thoughtful attention and opening your third inner ear to the leanings and feelings that lie like the music behind words. Listen between the lines and catch what is not said. Listen with your eyes, too, for so much communication is still non-verbal. Get clues from the tone, facial expressions, gestures, body language, etc.
- There are different levels of grasping. When a drop of water falls on a hot pan, it disappears instantly. If it falls on a lotus leaf, the lotus becomes more beautiful, though it will disappear with a bit of breeze. However, the same water drop converts into a pearl if it falls on an oyster. Be like an oyster.
- Be genuinely interested in what the speaker has to say. Have an open mind about what is being said. Leave behind your prejudices.
- Don't be under the false impression that you are intelligent enough to understand everything every time. This is a myth. Don't feel shy about admitting that you have not understood. Besides making a feedback-type physical response, a good listener also asks questions to clarify the information and test its validity. Repeat the message in your own words, and confirm whether you understood him correctly. Respond with encouraging verbal utterances such as yes, ok, or right. Respond by using encouraging non-verbal clues like nodding, leaning forward, and smiling. Don't be a miser in nodding. Nod frequently, as if you have Parkinson's disease. Nodding doesn't necessarily mean you agree with the speaker. However, keep in mind local practices for nodding. For

example, in India's southern region, what a particular nodding means is the opposite of what it means in the northern part.
- Listen patiently. Don't interrupt the speaker. Wait until the person is done speaking to respond. Interrupting a speaker is one of the most common discourteous acts.
- Don't frame counterarguments while listening. Listen to understand, not to reply.
- Listen to complaints. Whether complaints are made for the first or the tenth time, listen patiently and attentively. Be an empathetic listener rather than merely a sympathetic leader. See the problem from their point of view or frame of reference. Even if a complaint is unreasonable, don't brush it off. Allow him to tell his side of the story. Nod your head, ask questions, and get clarifications. Don't interrupt. Don't directly contradict. Instead, use a well-conceived, pointed question to highlight contradictions. When you do this, the person feels he was allowed to present his grievances, and sometimes all he wants is a patient hearing. Regardless of the resolution of his complaint, he will return satisfied.
- Watch your listen-to-talk ratio. Listen twice as much as you speak. Knowledge speaks, but wisdom listens. When you talk, you state what you already know, but you may know something new when you listen. When you listen to those you are surrounded by, you learn things you never knew before. Everyone you meet knows something you don't know. When you listen, you find that people who once appeared boring have valuable insights to offer. Be willing to learn from them. It is more profitable to be an attentive listener than a fluent speaker.
- Listen to your spouse attentively. Many marriages end in divorce primarily because the husband doesn't attentively listen to the wife, or vice versa.

APPENDIX 2

THE ART OF COMMUNICATION

- For seven out of ten minutes of our non-sleeping time, we communicate. The quality of our lives depends on the quality of our communication.
- Communication is the sister of leadership. Communication means imparting or exchanging information with others to secure the desired effect. Communication is a two-way process. Don't be an impersonal transmitter. Feel what you say, and your feeling should be one of caring. Feelings connect people. Also, communicate your inner thoughts, emotions, and spirit. Emotions mean energy in motion. Impart energy. Build up energy and enthusiasm for the work at hand. Shake up. Stir up. Inspire while you inform.
- Establish an emotional connection with the person you are communicating with. Engage him with the objective of developing a relationship beyond the current transaction. This will create a sense of belonging.
- Speak only when you are sure your words are better than silence. Sometimes, not saying anything is the answer. Though silence might be misunderstood as arrogance, no one can misquote it. Measure your words wisely. Calibrate your words carefully. Practice writing poems and essays; this will improve your word selection. Before you speak, your words should pass three tests. Is it necessary? Is it true? Is it kind and non-offensive? Test your words on yourself before using them for others. You cannot retract words once they leave your mouth. Sometimes, words may hurt more than a slap on the face. The tongue has no bones, but it is strong enough to break a heart. The life span of spoken words is longer than human life.
- Breathe your character through the sentences you speak.
- Talk at a slow speed. This will avoid possible speech distortions.
- Voice is the combination of the words you use and how you use them. It's one of the most powerful business tools around.
- Practice gradually decreasing your decibels. Low decibels bring divine serenity to your voice. Aim for whispering-level decibels. Never raise

your voice. High decibels don't mean your statement is true. In fact, the converse is true.
- Avoid monotony. Speak enthusiastically. Learn to make your tone pleasing.
- Prepare well. Be articulate and brief. Communicate using telegraphic language. Communicate like in television commercials, where they convey a high-impact message in less than thirty seconds.
- Use simple language. It should be direct and obvious.
- Talk to people at their level, using language they can relate to. Keep in view the perceptions, prejudices, and values of the recipient. Never talk about your riches amid the poor or about your children amid the barren.
- Prefer positive to negative statements. Start your conversation positively by saying, 'You have completed 90% of the task' rather than 'You didn't complete the task.'
- Call people by their first names. Pronounce names correctly. A man's name is very dear to him. One's name is like music to one's ears. In whichever language you call his name, it is the sweetest sound for him! Remembering and using someone's name is an instant rapport-builder and a solid foundation for great relationships.
- Talk face-to-face and assess the listener's comprehension through his facial expressions and body language. Maintain eye contact while talking. It is just as important as your speech, and it demonstrates truthfulness. Look fearlessly into the eyes of others. Remove your sunglasses if you are talking to anyone in the street. It is a sign of respect.
- Ask questions or seek opinions. This makes the other person feel important. Occasionally, ask questions, even if you know the answers.
- Communicate clearly and unambiguously. If anything can be misunderstood, it will be misunderstood. So devote a little more time and communicate correctly in the first place, rather than correcting the repercussions of misunderstandings.
- Once words are out of your mouth, how you are understood is what matters—not what was said or how it was said.
- 'I' is the most selfish single-letter word. Frequent use of 'I' reflects your ego and dampens the spirit of teamwork. 'I', 'me' and 'mine' bring so much attachment, leading you to identify with something and imparting

expression to the attachment. This makes your inner world much bigger than the external world, though the converse is reality. Hence, use 'We' more often than 'I'. Try to go through one full day without uttering 'I, me, or mine' in your communication, and then make this a habit.
- Four hard-to-say but very effective phrases are:
  - I don't know. -I was wrong.
  - I am sorry. -I need help.

- Learn to be soft-spoken. Make your conversation soft and palatable. The more knowledgeable the person, the softer he is in expressing his views. The more your communication is soft, the greater the probability of getting your work done. A wise leader won't say, 'I want this task to be done right now'. The other person can give several reasons, validly justifying why he can't do that right now. He would rather say, 'This task is urgent. I know you are too busy. Depending upon the urgency of other tasks you are preoccupied with, you may decide.' The most likely answer will be, 'I will do it right now, Sir.'
- Never order anyone. No one likes to receive orders—not even a two-year-old child. Don't even request it. Because even if you prefix the order or instructions with 'please' or convert those into a question form, it is still as good as an order, albeit a little less offensive. Instead, why not use the passive voice and thereby smartly avoid the tone of an order or even a request? For example, instead of saying:
  - 'File these papers' or
  - 'Please file these papers' or
  - "Could you file these papers?" or
  - "Could you please file these papers?"

say, 'These papers need to be filed.'

Your secretary will like this, and she herself will say, "I will file it, Sir." This is her own commitment, not your request or order. One's own commitment is more likely to be carried out than an order, even if the order is from the boss, who derives hierarchical authority from the employer-employee relationship. The most effective approach is to talk about what is required to be done and keep talking patiently. Your talk should inspire your staff to make a commitment on their own. Learn the art of getting people to do what you want them to do because they want to do it. Ignite the fire within them. Your Leadership Quotient can be considered high if you can extract the desired commitment from your followers without using your authority to issue orders. A wise boss never orders. He doesn't have hierarchical undertones. All he does is tell what is required to be done, and his followers are more than willing to cooperate. A good leader knows the secret to arousing his followers' willing and enthusiastic support. Under all conditions, human beings are most willing to obey those they believe to be the best. In sickness, people most readily obey the doctor. They don't question doctors' prescriptions. Aboard a flight, people obey the pilot. Thus, professional or technical competence is essential for a leadership position. Be the best in your field, and your followers will most readily obey you, eliminating the need for you to use your authority to impose orders.

- Even in restaurants, don't order, but request! Also, one more tip as a part of a good recipe for successful living is to mix a bit of a smile with the request.
- Make everyone feel that they are partners in the common enterprise. This is an index of the effectiveness of your communication.
- Anyone can hold the helm when the seas are calm. The critical test of the power of communication comes when the seas are rough and people feel disoriented and out of touch. Communicate hope when everyone around you doubts the promise of the future.

APPENDIX 3

THE ART OF ARTICULATED RESPONSES

Some people get offended even by ordinary situations in life. They have developed a habit of looking for an occasion to be offended. A news report, an economic downturn, a traffic jam, a rude stranger, a sneeze, a black cloud, or any cloud—just about anything will do to offend them. This happens because of a low level of awareness. We can eliminate the tendency to get offended by raising our level of awareness. Remember, we have the freedom to choose our response, and we can make a conscious choice and refuse to get offended. Be a person who refuses to be offended by anyone, anything, or any set of circumstances. Not being offended is a way of saying, 'I have control over how I am going to feel, and I choose to feel peaceful regardless of what I observe going on.' When we feel offended, we are practising judgment. We judge someone else to be stupid, insensitive, rude, arrogant, or inconsiderate. We become upset and offended by their conduct. We wear the hat of a judge and give our verdict. When we judge someone, we don't define them; we define ourselves. This shows our craving to judge others. A wise man will never judge others. He would merely observe. When we stop judging others and become observers, we will appreciate the value of inner peace and find ourselves free of the negative energy of resentment, leading to a life of contentment. A bonus is that we will find others much more attracted to us, leading to enriching relationships.

Also, we don't have to be upset with any person or situation because both are powerless without our reaction. If someone calls me a donkey, I don't become one. However, if I get worked up, roll up my sleeves, and fight with him, I become one, as I have accepted his comment. When we react to negative things, we accept them and invite them into our lives. Establish awareness in defencelessness. Unless I attain a deep level of awareness, I am merely adding years to my life—growing older but not becoming wiser.

> "Between (external) stimulus and (our) response, there is a space. In that space, is our power to choose our response. In our response lies our growth and freedom."
>
> — **Viktor E Frankl**

Humans have evolved from animals over millions of years. Animals have a primitive brain known as the reptilian brain or lizard brain. Animals inhabit a jungle, constantly facing the threat of death from other creatures. Their reptilian brain treats every stimulus as if it poses a threat to their survival. Hence, the instinctive tendency of the reptilian brain is to respond violently to any stimulus in order to save its life. Whereas animals have only reptilian brains, humans have two more brains: the paleomammalian or emotional brain (limbic system) and the neomammalian or rational brain (neocortex). The electronic signal of stimulus takes a quarter of a second to travel from the reptilian brain to the paleomammalian brain. If we respond to a stimulus instantly, our response will be animal-like. If we allow a quarter second to pass, our paleomammalian brain takes over control of the situation. Once the paleomammalian brain is activated, our response will be human-like. So, we should never translate our thoughts into action in anger. Allow a quarter of a second to pass. Handle this space by taking a deep breath, counting from one to ten, chanting some mantra, etc., thereby allowing the paleomammalian brain to take control of the situation. Thus, how we handle the space between external stimulus and our response determines the quality of our lives.

The situation is an external reality. Our reaction or response to that situation generated in our mind is an internal reality. Our internal dialogue, likes and dislikes, temperament, judgment, and preconceived notions constitute our internal reality. We should purify internal reality with enlightenment to view external reality in its unpolluted form and interpret it in its proper perspective. We don't have control over the situation coming to us, nor can we control the behaviour of others; but we have full control over our response. Our greatest inner strength is the power to be silent, the power to be calm. Our belief that life is full of infinite possibilities is our internal strength. This belief gives us ample scope for creative solutions. Our inner strength is a commitment to be a part of the solution.

APPENDIX 4

DEVELOPING ENRICHING RELATIONSHIPS IN GENERAL AND BUSINESS RELATIONSHIPS IN PARTICULAR

- Cultivate a people-focused culture.
- Forge and foster great friendships. Friendships are the backbone of an enriching and fulfilling life. A man's friendships are one of the best measures of his worth. Of all possessions, a friend is the most precious. Friendships are important both in personal and professional lives. If you want to walk fast, walk alone. But if you want to walk far, do so together. 'Don't worry; I am there' is a magical phrase that can rejuvenate a broken person. Such assurance by itself can work as a tonic, whether encashed or not.
- Keep all your relationships cordial. Relationships need curiosity to grow, candour to deepen, and integrity to continue.
- Celebrate in others their finest qualities. Treat them all in an 'as if' manner. Treating others in an 'as if' manner means visualising as if the qualities you are looking for already exist in them. You can accomplish this by simply changing your mind. Once you change your thoughts about relationships, you will respond according to your highest expectations. And gradually, you will see the rightness of your thoughts manifesting everywhere you go.
- In relationships, learn to see. Don't merely look. When you look through lenses of anger, hate, jealousy, and fear, you look more but see less. See more by removing all those negative lenses. Overlook the weakness of others. Thinking about others' imperfections is likely to irritate your mind. Leave their imperfections to them. Let them handle it. If you look for flaws, you will surely find them. Don't search for flaws using a magnifying glass. Instead, use a magnifying glass to search for as many good qualities in others as you can. Be mature enough to ignore the petty feelings of others.
- Having too many expectations from our relationships is often at the core of strained relationships.
- Realise that relationships function as mirrors and are governed by the Law of Reciprocity. Treat people the way you want to be treated. Don't

treat people the way you would not like to be treated. If someone does not treat you well, you are probably not treating him well. Hence, the only course of action is to change your behaviour.
- The relationship is about accepting each other as coal until diamonds form, not about finding gold or silver among the rocks of life.
- Start each day by asking, "How do I want others to feel?" Then act accordingly.
- Eliminate the 'I v/s you' or 'Us v/s them' mentality.
- Remember, you don't meet people by accident. Every person you meet will have a role in your life, big or small. Some will inspire you to do better, some will help you grow, and some may hurt you. Similarly, you are also playing some role in their lives. Know that paths cross for a reason, and hence, be kind to everyone.
- Remember, everyone has a story. Everyone has a past. People's behaviour depends on what they have gone through in the past or something they are still going through. Behaviour doesn't happen in a vacuum. Everyone has inner battles and issues. Some are a source of pride, and others are best left behind. But whatever their past, people do change and grow. Withhold your judgment about others. Instead of judging people based on their history, stand by them, help them build their future, and offer the same consideration you would like to receive. Never look down on someone unless you are helping them up. We think of life as a meritocracy, so we tend to look down on someone who isn't as successful, accomplished, or well-educated as we are. However, you may not know how far that person has already climbed in another field or where he will end up in the future. Time could easily reverse your positions, so treat everyone with dignity.
- Don't try to make yourself great by making someone else look small. The moment you think you have the right to belittle others because you feel you are better than they are, at that very moment, you become powerless.
- Create barriers to entry. Don't make yourself too accessible to everyone. Remain slightly aloof. The stars remain far above the earth. So keep a distance from all but your closest relations. Don't let everyone know everything about you. Cultivate a mystique. Judiciously balance working on the image you project to the rest of the world and your inner

character. Familiarity breeds contempt. Once people see everything about a leader, he loses his aura, as well as the authority and mystique he may have created. However, avoid arrogance.
- Don't meet a man you don't like. Don't get this wrong. Beyond its literal meaning, it emphasises the need to start liking every person you meet. That is the way you should feel about people. Can you strike a successful business deal with someone you don't like? And even if the deal is stuck, will it be executed successfully? Expand your circle and like every person you meet. This will enrich your life. Practice liking people until you develop a habit of doing so. People open up to you like a flower to the sun when you like them.
- Stay connected. Meet like-minded people regularly.
- Treat everyone you meet with honour and respect. Do so, even if they disrespect you. If anyone is rude, don't stoop to their level, but remain graceful and poised. Should you allow others to make you quit your good manners? Learn to respect all staff (including juniors), customers, vendors, and competitors. Respect is an investment that comes back to you together with compound returns. Respect should be visible, even in small gestures. Open the door for the people coming behind you, including juniors. You don't become small by treating others well.
- Be kind whenever possible. Also, remember that it is always possible. Treat everyone with kindness—not because they are kind-hearted, but because you are. Kindness toward others is one of the most valuable qualities. Kindness is the language that even the deaf can hear and the blind can see. Expressing kindness just needs a few words, and communicating the same may just need a few minutes, but their echoes are truly endless. Be kind to others, even those who are unkind to you. They need it even more. Your greatest test is how you deal with people who have mistreated you.
- Add a flavour of the human touch to all your interactions. Demonstrate sincerity, courtesy, kindness, and consideration to all your staff rather than a non-humane, mechanical, and selfish approach to getting your work done by any means. Respect them as people and respect their contribution, irrespective of what their role is. They appreciate courtesy from the boss and are quick to notice the lack of it, too. You can buy a man's time, physical presence, and a measured number of muscular

motions per hour, but you can't buy enthusiasm, initiative, loyalty, and devotion of heart, mind, and soul; you have to earn it. If you treat your men like machines, they will respond like machines, which means they will do just so much and no more. Conversely, if you show concern for them as human beings, they will feel obliged to help you and the organisation. Make them feel like they matter; they belong to you. Make them count, and let the evidence be visible to them. Avoid lip service. Demonstrate by your actions and behaviour that you mean what you say. Don't say you will do something unless you will indeed do it. Say only what you can do, and do what you say. This also applies to our business associates, customers, and vendors.

- Show a personal interest in the lives of your employees. Look after their welfare. Enquire about the welfare of their families. Remember their birthday and wedding anniversary dates, wish them well, and present gifts. If someone takes leave due to his wife's illness, inquire about her health when he returns. If someone walks with a limp, ask how it happened. Allow him to tell his story and exaggerate as much as he pleases. If someone has a personal problem affecting his mood or performance, be considerate and go out of your way to help him. If we have a caring heart, people will see it and perform better.
- Never miss an opportunity to congratulate anyone's achievement or, more importantly, express sympathy in sorrow or grief.
- Be courteous and polite at all times. However, never be pushed around. Ensure that you are always treated with respect.
- Don't laugh at others' dreams. Instead, encourage and inspire them to develop their vision. Help them reach a level higher than they ever would have imagined on their own. However, don't spoon-feed them. Instead, guide them to their source of power. Offer them support and motivation. Every person is born with a special ability. Just help him bring that to the world.
- Read people and influence the reading of yourself by others, and customise both for any personal or business situation. Don't get carried away by first impressions. Take a second look at the first impressions. We have an outward appearance—how we look, the clothes we wear, the car we drive, the house we live in, and the money we have. However, what really matters is our character. So dress up your body, but don't

forget to decorate your soul. An individual's exterior or outward forms are illusions. The reality lies in that which is esoteric—the inner part.
- Be close to your enemy, yet create a distance from him. If you notice a change in him, make sure it's not superficial.
- Life is not easy. It has to be made easy by patiently waiting, accepting whatever comes our way, bearing many things, and ignoring and overlooking many things. One of the mantras of our life should be ॐ इग्नोराय नमः:(Ohm ignorai namah). Life could be unfair to you at times. However, life's unfairness doesn't give you a license to walk the wrong path. Treat all people with love and compassion. Appreciate those who have supported you, forgive those who have hurt you, and help those who need you.

APPENDIX 5

INTERNAL AND EXTERNAL MEETINGS

- Critically examine the very need for a meeting. Instead of a meeting, consider a teleconference, videoconference, webinar, or circulating business or idea notebook.
- Apart from the meeting itself, the pre-meeting and post-meeting stages are also important. Plan and manage all the stages of the meeting to make it time-efficient and successful.
- Identify the meaningful purpose or theme of the meeting, like solving a problem or arriving at a decision, and categorise it accordingly so that planning and preparations are focused.
- Keep the direct and indirect costs of the meeting in mind all the time.
- Bunch your meetings.
- Cut meetings down to size—reduce the number of meetings you attend.
- Make a selective list of attendants who could contribute to the purpose as a resource person, like a technical expert, legal expert, or idea man. Optimise the number of participants. When you receive an invitation to participate in a meeting, ask what contribution is expected from you or ask, 'Can we not discuss this informally over a cup of coffee in your office?'
- Decide in advance when the meeting will start and end, and notify participants beforehand.
- Go for breakfast meetings or schedule the meeting before lunchtime or towards the end of the day to prevent it from dragging.
- To facilitate the conduct of the meeting in a time-efficient manner, decide on a suitable venue, seating arrangements, projection screen, etc. beforehand. Have all the gadgets checked before the meeting starts.
- Don't volunteer to hold a meeting in your room. Avoid becoming the meeting's host. Try to have it in someone else's room or conference room.

- Consider removing all chairs if you are looking to shorten the duration of the meeting.
- Prefer a seating arrangement in the shape of a round table that symbolises equality and induces team spirit. (During India's long freedom fight, three landmark meetings were organised on round tables and have been popularly described in history as the round table conferences.)
- Issue an agenda beforehand. Involve the participants by inviting comments and suggestions from them. Remind them again one day before the meeting date. This way, no one will indulge in adding a new point to the agenda during the meeting.
- Consider circulating relevant reading materials, popularly known as Approach Papers, along with the agenda. Invite participants to submit Approach Papers. Insist all participants read Approach Papers. Well-prepared Approach Papers can bring all the participants on the same page, making it easier to move forward in the desired direction.
- Itemise the issues you want to cover and present them as posers rather than statements. If issues are presented as statements, the participants are likely to harden their stand, thinking that the organiser of the meeting wants to dictate his pre-decided views. However, issues, when presented as posers and decided after deliberations, will have a stamp of consensus.
- Sequence the agenda in the proper order of importance and explain how you would like to cover it. Discuss vital items first. Start the meeting on a high note by taking up non-controversial items first.
- Allocate time for each agenda item based on its importance and inform the participants beforehand. Make someone responsible for each item on the agenda with an accountability mindset.
- Know the participants who are attending the meeting.
- If required, pre-speak individually and advocate for or lobby for your views. By pre-speaking, you nurture their egos and avoid possible knee-jerk reactions during the meeting.
- Identify and isolate anyone with conflicting views by either trying to get him on your side beforehand or mustering enough support to counteract such views.

- Diagnose and treat hidden agendas that influence participants' thinking and may prevent some from contributing.
- Use the meeting as an opportunity to meet and get to know the people you work with, especially if you work on a long-distance basis.
- Have the meeting audio or video recorded. However, you don't need to transcribe the audiotapes; simply keep them for future reference if necessary.
- Keep required stationery, extra copies of the agenda, and supporting or additional information likely to be needed in the meeting room.
- Prepare well for the meeting, and insist that participants come prepared.
- Despite late arrivals, start meeting on time. Avoid meeting tardiness. Minute absenteeism, late arrivals, and read when offenders are present. Collect a small sum, say $25, from latecomers and use the money accumulated for a weekend get-together.
- Do away with extended, aimless pleasantries.
- Start meeting briskly and make it impactful.
- Request the operator not to divert calls during the meeting.
- Demand a competent leader who can keep the meeting moving ahead briskly, everyone involved, and decisions being made.
- Avoid digressions yourself and control digression attempts by others.
- Keep meetings on target by using a board with a poser posted on it.
- Respect the chair. Speak with the permission of the chair. Don't interrupt others.
- Keep meetings free from arguments. Avoid debate over who is at fault for a delay or a mistake. Instead, such cat-and-dog fights get down to the business of the meeting.
- If you have to leave early, prepare the Chairman and others for this beforehand. Once you have completed the agenda relevant to you, request permission to leave. For this purpose, insist that agenda points relevant to you are bunched up together.
- If a need arises, hijack the chair and run the meeting yourself.
- Learn and practice the art of good Chairmanship. If you are chairing a meeting:
- Be a clear and rapid thinker, an attentive listener, impartial and impersonal, a referee and a leader, patient, tolerant, kind, friendly but brisk, and business-like.

- Establish ground rules for attendance, participation, and behaviour.
- A chairman should not speak much himself. He should just start the show.
- Don't worry if you are not a fluent speaker. What counts is your ability to put your case clearly in the meeting.
- Give positive or negative feedback by expression or movement of the head, body language, etc.
- Recognise and appreciate the contributions of participants.
- Control over participation by a few ego-driven, extrovert participants firmly but gracefully in a non-offensive manner.
- Give those who are less assertive, shy, or introverted an opportunity to speak. Prompt or provoke them to speak.
- Be cruel when some expert is invited to attend the meeting. He may throw his weight around and go on too long. Get an Approach Paper from him in advance. Then say, "Nice approach paper. Does anyone need to add anything?" in a firm tone of voice, obviously expecting a negative answer. If someone tries to object, use phrases like 'Has anybody any objection?' or 'Are you objecting? You are not. Right? Next business…' and the meeting can move on.
- Don't allow meetings to be used for discussing bilateral or personal issues or settling scores.
- Encourage participants to answer after careful thought and discourage the tendency to give off-the-cuff answers to impress others or to score points.
- Tighten focus with specific, pointed questions. Prevent it from becoming a disorganised forum.
- Keep track of the time. Keep reminding the participants about leftover time.
- Harness all available skills to arrive at a decision.
- Appoint one knowledgeable person to take the minutes. Consider preparing interim speed minutes covering only the decisions, assignments, and deadlines. Ensure everyone gets a rough copy of the speed minutes before they leave the meeting.
- Summarize frequently at small intervals.
- Wind up on a positive note. Conclude the meeting with an impactful punch that participants can remember as a takeaway from the meeting.

- If one more meeting is absolutely necessary, schedule the same before winding up when all are present.
- Promptly circulate the final minutes of the meeting, briefly covering the proceedings of the meeting and the decisions made and taking follow-up action.
- Focus on the human aspects of the meeting to reinforce the team spirit among the participants. Add richness to business life by having brief social talks before or after the meeting.
- To assess the real importance of a meeting, cancel or skip one or two scheduled meetings. Also, skip unproductive meetings or depute your assistant to attend the meeting.

APPENDIX 6

DETERMINING AND CERTIFYING DELAY DAYS: A TYPICAL EXAMPLE

Time overruns in the execution of construction projects are quite common. These time overruns are usually quite large in magnitude. Many construction projects take even double the time originally envisaged. The inherent peculiar characteristics of the construction projects make them highly vulnerable to time overruns. This issue assumes even more seriousness in the case of BOT projects because of the shear magnitude of their cascading effects. Presenting reasons for delays and getting them certified by an Independent Engineer or Employer is a herculean task.

One such BOT construction project was entangled in delays of unprecedented magnitude. It was quite challenging to approach the Independent Engineer and the Authority for the determination and certification of delay days. After a lot of brainstorming with the project team, a letter was prepared to present the case of the concessionaire. This letter is presented solely for educational purposes, duly masking project-specific details. Painstakingly refined after nearly a hundred iterations, the letter is a masterpiece, demonstrating business writing skills of the highest order. The structure of the letter, the language used, the words and phrases selected, the logical and chronological sequence of the cogent argument, the seamless flow, the tone delivered, etc. are all simply fabulous. The letter is comprehensive and complete in every aspect, including providing all enclosures, serial numbering, and binding them in three convenient volumes for easy reference.

Power-packed with all the ingredients that are required for an exemplary output, the letter could serve as the best example for reference. A valuable resource, the letter deserves preservation and is probably worth even being framed in a nice frame.

To,

The Independent Engineer,

Sub: Concession Agreement dated ... (**"Concession Agreement"** or **CA** in short) entered between ... (**"Authority"**) and ... (**"Concessionaire"**) for the ... road project on BOT (Annuity) basis—**Application for Determination and Certification of the number of days of delay in terms of Article 28.1 and other provisions of the Concession Agreement- Reg.**

Dear Sir,

1. The Concession Agreement (CA) for the above BOT (Annuity) Project under reference cited herein above was signed on ... The Appointed Date for the Project, as decided by the Authority, is ... As per Article 12.4.1 of the CA, the 910th day from the Appointed Date shall be the "Scheduled Four-Laning Date" (SFLD or SPCD) and accordingly, the Scheduled Four-Laning Date for the above Project is ...

2. SYNOPSIS

We wish to present herein below the synopsis of the Project in a chronological sequence covering major events commencing from the award of the Project:

2.1) Immediately upon receipt of the Letter of Award from the Authority, the Concessionaire diligently took up field survey work, geotechnical soil investigation work, preparation of designs and drawings, detailed scheduling and planning, etc.

2.2) The Concessionaire also started site mobilisation in the right earnest to undertake expeditious and fast-track implementation of the Project. Though even one camp at the center of the Site would have sufficed for this ... km-long stretch, the Concessionaire subdivided the Project Highway into three sub-stretches and treated each sub-stretch as a separate and independent unit. In order to attack all three sub-stretches simultaneously and concurrently, the Concessionaire established three Camps at ..., ... and ... Chainages.

Spread over about fifteen to twenty acres each, these camps had full-fledged establishments, including field offices, stores, mechanical workshops, field laboratories, staff and labour quarters, etc. A state-of-the-art casting yard for casting precast RCC girders was established at the camp with multiple casting beds and ... t capacity Gantry Crane for handling girders. Similarly, a fabrication yard with the required facilities for fabricating steel girders was established at ... camp. Facilities for casting precast RE wall panels were also established at multiple locations. In addition to the above three main camps, there were four sub-camps at various intermittent locations for stockpiling aggregate, GSB materials, WMM materials, sand, etc. The Concessionaire also invested huge money in procuring a fleet of Plant and Equipment and mobilised three independent sets of Plant and Equipment for accelerated implementation of the Project. In addition to the three sets of Plant and Equipment as above, standby Plant and Equipment were also provided for critical categories of Plant and Equipment so as to continue with the work uninterruptedly even if there are breakdowns of some Plant and Equipment.

As regards the supply of aggregate, since local manufacturers were not capable of supplying the required quantities as per the time schedule, nor a consistent quality of aggregate assured in their supplies, instead of depending upon such local suppliers, the Concessionaire made its own captive arrangement for bulk production of aggregate and established quarries at two locations so that uninterrupted supply of quality aggregate is ensured to suit the accelerated programme planned by the Concessionaire.

The list of major Plant and Equipment mobilised by the Concessionaire for the above three camps, four sub-camps and two quarries is enclosed as **Annexure 1**.

The above action on the part of the Concessionaire to plan and mobilise the site with three sets of Plant and Equipment together with standby Plant and Equipment of critical category clearly establishes sincere intention on the part of the Concessionaire to complete the Four-Laning much ahead of the Scheduled Four-Laning Date and to achieve COD prior to the Scheduled Four-Laning Date.

2.3) As regards the manpower, the Concessionaire mobilised over ... nos. of permanent category of staff, ... nos. of local staff and over ... nos. of skilled and unskilled labour.

2.4) Because of the above advance actions taken by the Concessionaire during the Development Period, the Concessionaire could commence physical activities at the Project Site immediately on the declaration of the Appointed Date.

2.5) In order to supplement in-house Project Management capabilities, the Concessionaire engaged M/s ... as Project Management Consultants. The PMC team of nearly ... members led by an expatriate Team Leader meticulously monitored the progress of the Project and continuously gave input and mid-course correction plans to the top Management for fast-track and accelerated execution of the Project for achieving COD prior to the Scheduled Four- Laning Date.

2.6) However, because of a variety of causes not attributable to the Concessionaire; the Construction Works could not proceed as per the accelerated programme planned by the Concessionaire (which was based on simultaneously attacking the Project from three sides with three sets of Plant and Equipment) and despite the Concessionaire having mobilised commensurate resources in abundance as stated above.

2.7) The main and primary cause of delay since the inception of the Project has been not providing vacant access and Right of Way to the Site on the Appointed Date, the Appointed Date plus 90 days and even thereafter for a substantially prolonged period, and the acquisition of land in several discontinuous stretches. Apart from the above primary cause, the performance of the Concessionaire was also affected by delays in obtaining approvals from Railways, a few Force Majeure events, and the introduction of a few Change of Scope (COS) Works ordered by the Authority that were required to be carried out during the Construction Period.

The Concessionaire has been bringing all these matters to the kind notice of the Independent Engineer (IE) and the Authority from time to time through various communication, discussions, and meetings, apart from periodically escalating this to the highest levels, and these are well documented on records.

2.8) While Construction Works were impeded by delays caused by Authority Event of Default, delays in procurement of approval from Railway authorities, Force Majeure Events and the introduction of COS Works during the Construction Period etc., the Concessionaire, on its part, went on executing Construction Works on whatever land that was made available to them at any given time. Since the pace of acquiring land was too slow, the Concessionaire, in order to engage its resources and reduce idling of resources, entered into personal negotiations with various landowners wherever possible, and because of such initiative and liaisoning effort on the part of the Concessionaire, the Concessionaire could open some more stretches for execution even though compensation was not paid by the Authority for those stretches. This liaisoning effort on the part of the Concessionaire not only helped the Concessionaire comply with the requirements set forth in Schedule G as regards the initial two Project milestones, viz. Project Milestones I and II, but also helped in achieving these two Milestones more than 60 days ahead of the Project Completion Schedule (viz. Schedule G of the CA). However, even after a lapse of 400 days of the construction period, the pace of land acquisition did not pick up. Eventually, the land acquisition issues became so acute that no more work fronts were available for engaging the Plant and Equipment of the Concessionaire despite continued liaisoning efforts on the part of the Concessionaire. This prevented the Concessionaire from achieving Project Milestone III which, of course, in any case, was rendered inapplicable because of inordinate delays in land acquisition and needed extension under and in accordance with the provisions of the CA.

2.9) The delays in land acquisition continued further and persisted not only right through the whole of the Construction Period but also even beyond the expiry of the Construction Period. Acknowledging the fact that even after a lapse of three and a half months past the expiry of the Construction Period, the Project was subjected to insurmountable hindrances at multiple places, the Authority, gave a directive to delink the above hindrance-affected portion and to put the rest of the stretch to Commercial Operations and gave consent to issue a Provisional COD on the above basis. Accordingly, based on the above directive and prior consent vide MOM dated ..., the IE declared Project Highway fit for entering into Commercial Operations on ... in terms of Article 10.3.5 of the CA and sought formal post-issuance approval from the Authority. On the above date, Four-lane traffic facility was available for as much as ... km out of ... km of Project length excluding hindered stretches and Bypass (i.e.,...%), albeit with a few discontinuities that were caused by inherent gaps in Land Acquisition and hindrances.

2.10) However, instead of giving post-issuance endorsement/approval for COD and commencing Annuity payments based on the IE's recommendations, surprisingly Authority decided to make further attempts for the elimination of discontinuities in land acquisition at this belated stage of the Project completely ignoring the cut-off date of Appointed Date plus 90 days stipulated in Article 10.3.5 of the CA and thereby went on compounding Authority Event of Default more and more.

2.11) Meanwhile, concerned about the recovery of the debt and interest thereon because of the non-commencement of Annuity payments despite the recommendation by IE, the Lenders did slowdown / stop funding for the Project.

2.12) Though funding was slowed down / stopped by the Lenders, the Concessionaire went on pumping its own funds and eliminated discontinuities as and when the Authority provided the land and removed hindrances in some of the discontinuities. Upon elimination of the discontinuities, once again, the IE recommended COD on ... However, the Authority kept on insisting on a continuous stretch of 41 km from the viewpoint of toll collections.

2.13) However, even after a lapse of 2148 days beyond Appointed Date, when land acquisition issues in a thickly populated, busy, and highly encumbered market area and two other discontinuities remained unresolved and when it was realised that providing land for four-laning of a continuous stretch of even ... km is not possible, a high-level meeting was convened on ... by the Ministry and discontinuities at the market area and at the other two locations were allowed for the purpose of COD.

2.14) Eventually, the PCOD was issued by the IE only on ... (i.e. on 2213rd day from Appointed Date) after obtaining fresh consent from the authority, and this consent was given only when Project Highway became toll-worthy, toll notification was published in newspapers, a toll collecting agency was appointed through e-tendering and the toll could be started.

2.15) Thus, the delay in achieving COD was caused firstly by abnormal delays in land acquisition and acquiring the same in several discontinuous stretches and secondly by not endorsing post-issuance approval to IE's COD recommendation under Article 10.3.5 of the CA on account of discontinuities and the Authority's apprehension about possible protests from road users regarding payment of road User Fees. You will kindly appreciate from the foregoing that the delay in achieving COD was caused by reasons not attributable to the Concessionaire. You will also agree that the above delay in the issue of COD is of unprecedented magnitude.

3. PROVISIONS OF CA

Article 34.6.2 of the CA stipulates that the Concession Period and the dates set forth in the Project Completion Schedule shall be extended by a period equal in length to the duration for which the Force Majeure Event subsists while as per Article 16.2.2 of the CA, the impact of COS Works on Project Completion Schedule needs to be determined if COS Works are required to be carried out during the Construction Period.

Further Article 28.1.3 of the CA, stipulates that the number of days by which COD preceded the Scheduled Four-Laning Date shall also include, as certified by the Independent Engineer, the aggregate number of days of delay caused by:

   I. Suspension or stoppage of Construction Works or part thereof by the Authority or the Independent Engineer, for reasons not attributable to the Concessionaire.
   II. Force Majeure Event, which is a Political Event and
   III. Authority Event of Default.

Article 35.2 of the CA, stipulates payment to the Concessionaire, by way of compensation, all direct costs suffered or incurred by the Concessionaire.

4. APPLICATION FOR DETERMINATION AND CERTIFICATION OF DELAY DAYS

As per MOM of the meeting held on ..., the decision on delay days is to be taken based on the recommendation of IE and accordingly, we hereby submit our Application for Determination and Certification of the number of days of delays by IE in terms of Articles 34.6.2, 16.2.2 and 28.1 of the CA.

As stated above, various causes of delay are already on record, which have now been consolidated and briefly presented in para 5 to 11 herein below in a chronological manner, duly grouping them appropriately for the purpose of Determination and Certification of the number of days of delays in terms of Articles 34.6.2, 16.2.2 and 28.1 of the CA and the compensation payable to the Concessionaire as per the provisions of the CA:

5. DELAYS ARISING DUE TO NOT PROVIDING VACANT ACCESS AND RIGHT OF WAY BY THE AUTHORITY: EXISTING NH EXCLUDING BYPASS AND ROBs

In this regard, we wish to submit the following:

5.1) For this BOT (Annuity) Project, the Authority has granted the Concession to the Concessionaire vide Article 3.1.1 of the CA and accordingly, Article 3.1.2(a) of the CA entitles the Concessionaire to Right of Way, access and license to the Site for the purpose of and to the extent conferred by the provisions of the CA.

5.2) The Authority has Represented and Warranted to the Concessionaire under Article 7.2 (j) of the CA that it has a good and valid right to the Site and has power and authority to grant a license in respect thereto to the Concessionaire.

5.3) Reference is kindly invited to Article 4.1.2 (a) of the CA, which stipulates that the Authority shall provide to the Concessionaire the Right of Way to the Site in accordance with the provisions of Article 10.3.1; provided that the conditions set forth in Article 10.3.2 shall also be satisfied on or prior to the Appointed Date. Article 10.3.2 of the CA implies that on or prior to the Appointed Date, the Authority shall have granted vacant access and

Right of Way for not less than 50% of the total area of the Site required and necessary for the Four-Lane Project Highway. This is a fundamental obligation of the Authority.

5.4) Article 10.4 of the CA requires that the Site shall be made available by the Authority to the Concessionaire free from all Encumbrances and occupations.

5.5) As per Article 10.2.3 of the CA, the license, access and Right of Way granted by the CA to the Concessionaire shall always be subject to existing rights of way, and it further states that the Concessionaire shall perform its obligation in a manner that two existing lanes of the Project Highway or an alternative thereof are open to traffic at all times during the Construction Period.

5.6) As per Article 4.5 of Annexure-I (Schedule-B) and Appendix BV, the widths of the proposed ROW in the existing lanes of Project Highway, Bypass, and Toll Plaza are 45 m, 60 m, and 110 m, respectively.

5.7) However, contrary to Representations and Warranties made by the Authority to the Concessionaire and various other provisions stipulated in the CA, the actual status of providing vacant access and Right of Way was quite different from what had been envisaged and stipulated in the CA, and the land was not acquired as per the provisions stipulated in the CA nor the land was provided in continuous/ contiguous manner but acquired land had several inherent discontinuities and hindrances, and these delays persisted for a substantially prolonged period beyond the cut-off date of Appointed Date plus 90 days stipulated in the CA as can be seen from the facts narrated in subsequent paras of this letter.

5.8) For recording an inventory of the Site in terms of the provisions of Article 10.3.1 of the CA, the Concessionaire requested the Authority Representative for a joint inspection of the Site vide letter dated ... **(Ref. 1)**.

5.9) Though it is expressly agreed in the CA that not less than 50% of the total area of the site required and necessary for Four-Laning is to be provided on Appointed Date, vacant access and Right of Way to only ... Hect. land was provided out of ... Hect. land required and necessary for four-laning as shown in **Annexure 2,** which in terms of the length is only … Km on LHS and … Km on RHS and that too was in several discontinuous stretches as shown pictorially in **sheet 2 of Annexure 2**.

5.10) As per Article 10.3.4 of the CA, the Authority is to make the best efforts to provide and grant the Right of Way to the Concessionaire in respect of all land not provided on the Appointed Date. However, as on the Appointed Date plus 90 days, only … Hect. land i.e. … Km on LHS and … Km on RHS was provided by the Authority and that too was in several discontinuous stretches, as shown pictorially in **Annexure 3**.

5.11) As stated above, even the land that was acquired and provided to the Concessionaire was not in a continuous/ contiguous stretch. As you are aware, road projects require a continuous stretch of a certain minimum length (say, at least 10 km, if not more) for time and cost efficiency of operations. However, on this Project continuous stretch of even 2 or 3 km was not provided, and as a consequence, the Concessionaire was compelled to alter the timing and sequencing of various construction activities. The Concessionaire had to keep shifting Plant and Equipment from one location to another repeatedly. This repeated back-and-forth shifting of Plant and Equipment drastically reduced its productivity, and to compensate for this reduced productivity, the Concessionaire kept on augmenting more and more resources. Furthermore, it's clear that the inherent discontinuities during land acquisition would lead to corresponding discontinuities in Four-Laning upon completion of the Project Highway on available land.

5.12) Also, even two existing lanes of the Project Highway were surrounded by shops, dhabas, hutments, electrical poles, etc. just at the edges on one or both sides (especially on the left side), thereby giving no room for traffic diversions required and necessary for taking up four-laning work and for keeping two existing lanes of the Project Highway open to traffic at all times during the Construction Period which is the Concessionaire's mandatory obligation under the CA.

5.13) Also, for any given stretch, land was not provided for the whole width of the ROW covering both LHS and RHS, but the land acquisition of LHS portion was done separately from RHS portion in different time spans.

5.14) Further, even whatever land was acquired and handed over had inadequate ROW width, whereby the construction of shoulders, toe drains, service roads, etc. could not be undertaken, and at some locations, even full median/carriageway was not possible, leading us to revise the designs and reduce median or provide restricted carriageway in consultation with the IE. In view of the above, in any given stretch we could not execute shoulders, toe drains, etc. simultaneously along with the carriageway, but we had to come back in that particular stretch to execute shoulders, toe drains, etc. after completing the carriageway, involving substantial reimbursable extra costs as well as time.

5.15) Also, the delay in land acquisition of the Main Carriage Way portion resulted in the Concessionaire requiring to repeatedly maintain Service Roads because Main Carriage Way traffic was continuously plying on the Service Road for a prolonged period, e.g. in the case of ... village, since Main Carriage Way hindrance persisted for a very long period, up and down traffic was plying on Service Road till Main Carriage Way could be completed. Similarly, in many stretches, because of hindrances on one side, four-lane traffic has been continuously plying on the completed two lanes of the other side, requiring periodic maintenance, e.g. ... km to ... km stretch. Kindly note that both up and down traffic has been plying in the completed portion of Carriage Way on RHS for the last four years. There are many such stretches where repeated periodic maintenance is required to be done.

5.16) The actual status of Vacant access and Right of Way provided to the Concessionaire was recorded in our letter dated ... **(Ref. 2)**.

5.17) Frustrated by prolonged and persisting delays in providing vacant access and Right of Way to Site, the Concessionaire issued a Notice to the Authority under Article 37.2.1 of the CA on ... **(Ref. 3)**. The Concessionaire stated that non-fulfilment of this basic and fundamental obligation by the Authority has caused Material Adverse Effect on the Concessionaire, causing Material Financial burden, and requested the Authority to cure this default within a Cure Period of 90 days. However, even after allowing for a Cure Period of 90 days, no progress was made in providing vacant access and Right of Way to the Site, nor any time schedule given by the

Authority as to when vacant access to the Site and Right of Way in balance areas will be provided or when discontinuities existing in acquired land will be eliminated. As a consequence of the above material default on the part of the Authority, the accelerated programme of the Concessionaire got completely thrown out of gear, and commensurately ample resources mobilised by the Concessionaire remained idle/unutilised. The Concessionaire, in order to engage its resources and reduce the idling of resources, entered into personal negotiations with various landowners wherever possible. With this initiative and liaisoning effort on the part of the Concessionaire, the Concessionaire could open some more stretches for work even though compensation was not paid by the Authority for those stretches. Though this liaisoning could not help the Concessionaire in achieving progress as per the accelerated programme planned by the Concessionaire, these efforts, coupled with the mobilisation of ample resources by the Concessionaire helped in achieving Project Milestones I and II earlier than specified in Schedule G of the CA. However, when there were no signs of payment of compensation to landowners, those landowners who had permitted the commencement of earthwork, GSB or WMM became restless, and stopped allowing the continuation of further layers, apprehending that if all layers were allowed to be completed, the compensation would never be paid to them, and accordingly, the Concessionaire could not carry on with the Work and thus was prevented from achieving Project Milestone III.

Of course, despite the partial engagement of resources as above, the resources of the Concessionaire did remain idle/unutilised and the Concessionaire had to continue to maintain its camps and fleet of Plant and Equipment, labour, staff etc. for a substantially prolonged period.

5.18) A jointly signed Memorandum of Inventory pursuant to Article 10.3.1 of the CA is enclosed **(Ref. 4)**.

5.19) As per provisions of the CA, the Vacant access and Right of Way available on Appointed Date and Appointed Date plus 90 days alone are relevant. However, we have also compiled information pertaining to subsequent periods, and the same is furnished, duly summarised on a monthly basis vide enclosed **Annexure 4**. The purpose of this compilation is only to show the extremely slow pace of acquiring land.

5.20) You will kindly observe from the above Annexure, that, apart from the fact that on Appointed Date only ... land was provided out of ... Hect. land required and necessary for four-laning, the pace of acquiring ROW even after the Appointed Date was quite slow, and the delays persisted for substantially prolonged periods even beyond the cut-off date of the Appointed Date plus 90 days.

5.21) A joint inspection was carried out by the IE and the Concessionaire on ... to ascertain the status of the availability of the Site for Project Execution. This is recorded in a letter dated ... **(Ref. 5).** The IE requested the Authority to take the necessary action for the availability of the balance land.

5.22) A copy of the Strip Chart showing the status of hindrances as on ... was forwarded to the Authority by IE vide letter dated ... **(Ref. 6).** The IE requested that the Authority to take suitable action for the removal of the hindrances so that work can be undertaken at those stretches at the earliest.

5.23) There were many fundamental reasons why the Authority could not provide vacant access to the site. These reasons included poor records of land ownerships, substantial delays in payment of compensation to landowners, substantial delays in measurements of structures and payment of suitable compensation thereof, arbitrary classification of land in agriculture, residential and commercial categories, frequent re-classification of categories, not attending to issues raised by the landowners and allowing it to convert into a big agitation, delays in arbitration awards for land payment by the Administration, non-acceptance of arbitration awards by the Authority and challenging the same, and thereby triggering tedious legal process, landowners approaching DLAO court and High Court for adjudication of compensation matter, delays in Authority making payment for shifting electrical poles etc.

5.24) The magnitude and severity of the difficulties faced by the District Administration and the Authority in obtaining vacant access can be appreciated by the fact that the District Administration and the Employer had to periodically conduct several demolition drives accompanied by armed Police force amidst stiff local resistance to make available vacant access to some of the stretches, a few of which are shown in TABLE 1 :

Though four-lane traffic was running in many of the stretches since ..., non-clearance of the above hindrances, despite the use of the armed police force, caused discontinuities in four-laning in otherwise completed stretches. It is noteworthy that despite various demolition drives conducted by Authority/ Dist. Administration using Police protection, hindrances could not be eliminated.

5.25) You will also observe from **Annexure 4** that providing vacant access to the Site for Construction Works continued to remain in deficit even till the Scheduled Four-Laning Date i.e. ... and in fact, on the said SPCD, the Authority could acquire and provide only ... Hec. of the Site out of the total ... Hec. to be acquired and provided to the Concessionaire. The Land acquisition status on SPCD and the corresponding Strip Chart are shown in **Annexure 5**. Thus, this is a unique Project in which even when the Construction Period expired, substantial land was yet to be acquired, and these abnormal delays in providing vacant access and Right of Way had thrown the entire schedule, planning and costing of the Concessionaire out of gear. This being Material Default by the Authority, the Concessionaire is entitled to all reliefs and remedies as provided under the CA, including, Article 28.1, Article 35.2 and Article 35.3 etc.

5.26) The Concessionaire went on to complete four-laning in available areas and made four-lane traffic through in areas where vacant access and Right of Way was provided. The facility, thus constructed by the Concessionaire was put to use for its intended purpose, and the four-lane traffic on many of these stretches has been flowing continuously since ... giving much-needed relief to commuters of this prestigious stretch of National Highway as well as to the local residents of this area. In fact, the travelling time between these points has drastically reduced to 45 to 60 minutes since ..., as opposed to over three hours during pre-four-laning times.

5.27) Notwithstanding the fact that as on Appointment Date + 90 days, vacant access and Right of Way to only ... km on LHS and ... km on RHS was provided to the Concessionaire and that too was in several discontinuous stretches, before formally approaching the IE for a Provisional Certificate of Completion in March 2013, the Concessionaire completed substantially more areas than said lengths of … km and … km on LHS and RHS, respectively. The formal application for a Certificate of Completion under Articles 14.3 and 10.3.5 of the CA was submitted by the Concessionaire on … **(Ref 13).** Full sets of COD-related documents were also submitted along with the said application by the Concessionaire. It may be noted that even as late as in …; there were major insurmountable hindrances at multiple locations. However, barring the above locations where delay on account of hindrances was still continuing, the Concessionaire made four-lane traffic through in areas where vacant access and Right of Way was provided.

5.28) Subsequent to the aforementioned application, the Concessionaire submitted a reminder request on … **(Ref. 14)** to IE for the issuance of a Provisional Certificate of Completion under Article 10.3.5 of the CA. Though the cut-off date as per CA is the Appointed date plus 90 days, the Concessionaire submitted a list showing hindrances on LHS as well as RHS of the Project Highway existing even on that date, which was only to highlight the fact that delays in land acquisition persisted even after 995 days past Appointed Date.

5.29) Also, even at this belated stage of the Project, local agitation was continuing for suitable compensation, as can be seen from the videography submitted to the Authority on … **(Ref. 15).**

5.30) In order to discuss the COD application submitted by the Concessionaire and to review the land acquisition status for balance land, a high-level meeting was convened on … where all concerned were present.

Acknowledging the fact that even after a lapse of three and a half months past the expiry of the Construction Period, the Project was subjected to insurmountable hindrances at multiple locations; the Authority gave a directive to delink the above hindrance-affected portion and to put the rest of the stretch to Commercial Operations and gave consent to issue a Provisional COD on the above basis.

The minutes of the above meeting were recorded and circulated on ... **(Ref. 16)** which is partly reproduced below:

"IE/ Concessionaire may prepare the details of the works required at the site so that the project stretch between ... to ... can be safely and reliably put to Commercial Operation.

The above works are to be completed by ...; subsequently, the COD proposal duly recommended may be forwarded to the Authority HQ at the earliest."

Accordingly, based on the above directive of delinking the hindrance-affected portion and the prior consent to issue COD, the IE declared Project Highway fit for entering into Commercial Operations on...

For the sake of simplicity in presentation, the Bypass is presented in para 6 below followed by three ROBs which have been presented separately in para 7.1 to and 7.2 and 7.3 respectively, after which the presentation on PCOD recommendation and subsequent events are resumed and continued in para 8 and 9 in a chronological sequence.

6. DELAYS ARISING DUE TO NOT PROVIDING VACANT ACCESS AND RIGHT OF WAY BY AUTHORITY: BYPASS

6.1) As stated in para 2 above, the Concessionaire established a separate and exclusive camp for the Bypass with an independent and dedicated set of Plant and Equipment though the Bypass stretch was only 16.8 km long. Though the Concessionaire mobilised ample resources as above, this resource mobilisation could not be used effectively because of delays in providing vacant access and Right of Way in the Bypass.

6.2) Bypass being a fully green field stretch, it is all the more important that vacant access is made available on or prior to the Appointed Date and also without any discontinuity. However, even for this small green field stretch of ... km in length, vacant access was provided belatedly, and that too was in several discontinuous stretches, as can be seen from **Annexures 2 and 3**. Also, land at initial chainages at both ends of the bypass was not acquired, because of which the Concessionaire could not work as per the proper sequence.

6.3) Initially, few landowners demanded suitable compensation as per commercial rates which was not attended to by the Administration/Authority and authority. As a result, the landowners intensified their agitation and roped in other landowners, and eventually, it became a big agitation involving groups of activists like Kisan Morcha. Gradually, they completely stopped all works in the bypass, as can be seen from the events described below:

a) On ..., hundreds of farmers under a local leader met DM to present the demand for suitable compensation. Even DM appreciated the genuineness of the grievances of farmers and publicly announced that justice should be done to farmers by giving commercial compensation to them. This agitation was reported in a local daily newspaper dated ... **(Ref. 17).**

b) On ..., DM organised Janta Darbar at ... to hear the grievances of land owners affected by the bypass works. Landowners submitted around 200 representations. This agitation was reported in a local daily newspaper dated ... **(Ref. 18).**

c) On ..., landowners stopped the bypass work. Over a dozen trucks of the Concessionaire were taken into their custody. Representatives of the Concessionaire explained to the villagers, but in vain. Only after the intervention of DM were the trucks released. This agitation was reported in a local daily newspaper dated ... **(Ref. 19).**

d) On ..., bypass work was stopped by villagers who manhandled labours. Upon intervention by the local leader and his assurance that he would take up the matter with DM, the agitation was called off. Villagers demanded compensation at commercial rates. This agitation was reported in a local daily newspaper dated ... **(Ref. 20).**

6.4) Though the DM, himself along with his team visited the bypass location several times to persuade the landowners, the issue of land compensation could not be resolved and eventually the Administration had to arrest many local people who were at the forefront of the protest.

6.5) When the District Administration/Authority could not resolve compensation issues despite repeated promises made by the DM, the landowners became impatient and intensified their agitation further, and started violent protests. Eventually, the landowners completely halted all the works in the bypass from ... Their demand included the provision of an Underpass at ... apart from the payment of compensation as decided by the DM. This stoppage of work was notified vide letter dated ... **(Ref. 21)**.

6.6) It can be seen from the enclosed **Annexure 6** that the Concessionaire has completed the DBM layer in as much as ... km in LHS and ... km in RHS before work was completely stopped in Bypass, notwithstanding the fact that working with several discontinuities as above involved huge reimbursable additional costs. As regards culverts, the Concessionaire completed all culverts in the bypass where Vacant Access and Right of Way were provided.

6.7) The agitation of landowners is continuing even now, as can be seen from our letter dated ... **(Ref. 22),** when local landowners registered a protest during the public meeting of the Hon'ble Minister.

7. DELAYS ARISING DUE TO NOT PROVIDING VACANT ACCESS AND RIGHT OF WAY BY AUTHORITY AND DELAYS IN PROCURING RAILWAY APPROVAL

There have been inordinate delays in procuring the railway's approvals. This can be observed from the enclosed documents (**Ref. 23** to **Ref. 39**).

8. ISSUE OF PCOD UNDER ARTICLE 10.3.5 OF THE CA AND SUBSEQUENT DEVELOPMENTS

8.1) Upon determining the Tests (conducted as per Article 14.1) to be successful as per Article 14.3, and having been satisfied that the Project Highway can be safely and reliably placed in the commercial service of the Users thereof, the IE declared Project Highway fit for entry into Commercial Operations on ... and issued a Provisional Certificate of Completion vide letter dated ... **(Ref. 40),** according to which the Commercial Operations Date of the Project is ... and the Concessionaire is entitled to receive Annuity from the Authority in accordance with the provisions of Article 15.1 read with Article 27.1 and 27.2. The IE confirmed that an unhindered ROW of only ... Km on LHS and ... on RHS was provided to the Concessionaire on Appointed Date plus 90 days and considering the hindrances still existing on the NH-77 as well as the bypass, recommended an extension of the Construction Period up to ... The IE also confirmed that out of ... project length, excluding hindered stretches and bypass, four-lane traffic facilities are available for a length of ... (i.e. ... %). However, the IE restricted declaring Provisional Certificate of Completion only for ... Km stretch (i.e. from km ... to km), which was almost continuous, although in addition, further ... Km in two stretches (i.e. from km ... to km ... and km ... to km ...) were also completed, and four-lane traffic was operating but was not included in PCOD stretch because of intervening gaps of one km each.

The issue of the above PCOD by the IE and seeking formal post-issuance approval from the Employer was in line with the directives and prior consent given by the Authority during the meeting held on ... and MOM thereof.

8.2) However, the formal post-issuance approval of PCOD by the Employer got delayed because of a series of back-and-forth correspondences. The above delay resulted in a slowdown or stoppage of funding by the Lenders and an increase in interest payments on the debt, an increase in capital costs on account of inflation, and an increase in other costs.

8.3) The Authority gave certain comments on ... **(Ref. 41)** which were replied to para-wise by the IE vide letter dated ... **(Ref. 42)**. The IE stated that the Supplementary Agreement shall be signed with the Concessionaire for the completion of balance items, as it would be contractually prudent to take these items out of the present the CA to avoid granting Extension of Concession Period consequent to a delay in the completion of these works where non-availability of land and hindrances still existed.

8.4) The Authority forwarded the recommendation of the IE to the Regional Office on ... **(Ref 43)** stating therein that the IE has issued a Provisional Completion Certificate for a part length of the Project Highway for which there is no clarity in the CA, and the proposal was forwarded for further necessary action.

8.5) The Regional Officer of the Authority forwarded the Certificate issued by the IE to HQ on ... **(Ref. 44)** stating inter alia in para 4.1 that the Project Highway has been provisionally declared fit for entry into Commercial

Operation on ... by the IE and though the SPCD was ..., no damages for delay are attributable to the Concessionaire as completion was delayed because of a delay in handing over the land. RO stated that there have been hindrances by the landowners demanding higher compensation, because of which encumbrance-free land could not be handed over to the Concessionaire. On the other hand, the RO also expressed apprehension that although the total length under provisional COD is 31.112 Km, the stretch has discontinuities because of land acquisition issues, and therefore the road users may not accept the levy of the user fee. This was apprehended because facilities were incomplete at both ends of the provisionally completed stretch apart from a few discontinuities in between. However, notwithstanding the above discontinuities, RO also recommended considering the issue of a Provisional COD so that project completion (of balance works) is not affected because of the non-availability of finance.

8.6) Though the IE issued COD on ... and even RO requested HQ to consider COD as issued by the IE, HQ chose not to endorse the same on account of discontinuities. During each follow-up meeting, HQ kept on assuring that COD would be endorsed, but the same was not done in gross violation of the provisions of the CA.

8.7) Subsequently, HQ communicated comments vide letter dated ... **(Ref. 45)** on the aforesaid proposal by IE and sought to resubmit the proposal with the details requested therein.

8.8) The comments were forwarded to the IE and the Concessionaire for reply, and the Concessionaire provided the reply vide letter dated ... **(Ref. 46)** and further added that in view of the delay in commencing Annuity payments, the Lenders have slowed down / stopped funding the Project and in the meanwhile the Concessionaire had no option but to pump in its own funds for the execution of balance Works and that such a situation cannot continue for long. The Concessionaire highlighted the fact that for proceeding with the balance Works in full swing, obviously finance by the Lenders is a must. However, even after a lapse of considerable time beyond SPCD and a lapse of as much as ... days after the date of IE issuing the PCOD certificate, the Annuity was not commenced, nor was the Project

Highway free of hindrances even at this belated stage of the Project. The Concessionaire once again drew the attention of all concerned to Article 10.3.5 of the CA and requested the Authority to endorse the PCOD Certificate issued by the IE which was entangled in a series of back-and-forth correspondences.

8.9) The IE furnished para wise reply vide letter dated **(Ref. 47)** to the queries raised by the Authority and requested further necessary action on the basis of the comments thus furnished.

8.10) Meanwhile, hindrances not vacated till as late as … were recorded vide letter dated … enclosing the strip chart therein **(Ref. 48)**.

8.11) The Concessioner again reminded IE vide letter dated … **(Ref. 49)** that despite the issue of COD by the IE, Annuity payments have not been commenced, leading to a slowdown or stoppage of funding by Lenders. During the meeting held on …, it was agreed that hindrances would be removed within a week. However, hindrances could not be removed. The Concessionaire further stated that multiple hindrances still exist at the Project Site, which are resulting in the non-elimination of discontinuities and also delays in the completion of balance works. The Concessionaire also stated that in the meeting with the Authority, it was agreed by the Authority that before …, the issue of determination of delay days will also be finalised along with the grant of a Provisional COD.

8.12) Reference is invited to the IE's letter dated … **(Ref. 50),** which confirms that hindrances on discontinuous patches have not been removed to date except for a few minor patches. This was the status of the removal of hindrances on … days after the issue of PCOD and 1310 days after the Appointed Date. It may be noted that the COD issued by the IE was not endorsed on the ground of discontinuity, which existed even after a lapse of 1310 days beyond the Appointed Date, though the provisions of the CA very clearly stipulate that land for which Vacant Access and Right of Way were not provided even on Appointed Date plus 90 days shall not come in the way of COD. However, in this project, PCOD was not endorsed by the Authority on account of discontinuity, which was not removed even after a lapse of 1310 days beyond the Appointed Date which grossly violates the provisions of the CA and is highly unjust. You will kindly observe a gross contradiction in the stand taken by the Authority. PCOD issued by IE was not endorsed because of discontinuities, and those discontinuities were present even after a lapse of 1310 days past Appointed Date!

8.13) The Authority informed, vide letter dated ... **(Ref. 51)** that during the meeting held on ..., it was decided that the Concessionaire will make best efforts to complete all discontinuities by ... because it was apprehended that road users may resist levy of user fee on account of discontinuities and hence PCC could not be issued. The Authority accordingly requested the IE to again send a fresh / revised PCOD proposal after the elimination of discontinuities.

8.14) The Concessionaire reiterated vide letter dated ... **(Ref. 52)** that the Concessionaire had completed a substantially larger stretch than that were provided by the Authority on the Appointed Date plus 90 days. However, during the meeting held on ..., some more areas were identified for inclusion in the COD stretch - vacant access to some of which was provided to the Concessionaire as late as ... The Concessionaire stated that as per Article 10.3.5 of the CA issue of a Provisional Certificate shall not be affected or delayed on account of Vacant Access to any part of the site not being granted or any construction on such part of the site remaining incomplete on the date of tests on account of the delay or denial of such access thereto even on Appointed Date plus 90 days and the Concessionaire once again requested the Authority to endorse Provisional Certificate of Completion w.e.f. ... together with determination and certification of number of days by which COD preceded the Scheduled Four-Laning Date including aggregate number of days of delay as per Article 28.1 of the CA so that Lenders can resume funding.

8.15) Meanwhile, even at this belated stage of the Project, the local landowners were continuing their demands for suitable compensation and were becoming big obstacles in the elimination of discontinuities and completion of balanced Construction Works. To cite an example, the Concessionaire started the work at Toll Plaza through its own liaisoning and efforts, though land was not acquired. Subsequently, when compensation was not paid even after inordinate delays, the villagers and farmers complained that they had not received compensation payment and that work had commenced. They warned that a law and order situation may arise. This was reported in a newspaper dated … **(Ref. 53)**.

8.16) It is evident from the facts narrated in the foregoing that, despite being in Material Default, the Authority declined to take any cognisance of the provisions of the CA and chose not to endorse the Certificate issued by the IE. Consequently, Annuity payments were not commenced in gross violation of the provisions of the CA and in particular, Article 10.3.5. PCOD duly issued by the IE was not endorsed by the Employer, probably because of the presence of a few discontinuities and misconceptions at the field level of the Authority between completion as per the CA and completion for the purpose of tolling. As regards discontinuity, it was highly disturbing to note that, on one hand, the Employer was unable to provide vacant access and Right of Way to the Site in a continuous stretch, even several months past the cut-off date of the Appointed Date plus 90 days; on the other hand, the Employer did not commence Annuity payments on the grounds of discontinuity, which did exist even at that belated stage of the Project. If handed over land has inherent discontinuities, obviously the Concessionaire cannot make the road continuous. Thus, the discontinuities were not on account of the Concessionaire but were because of inherent discontinuities in land acquisition. Therefore, it was highly unjust on the part of the Employer to hold back PCOD already issued by the IE. The non-endorsement of PCOD issued by the IE on the grounds of discontinuity put the Concessionaire in an extremely difficult situation vis-a-vis Lenders of the Project. Moreover, because of the non-commencement of Annuity, there was a huge increase in interest payments on debt, a substantial increase in capital costs on account of inflation, and an increase in other costs.

As regards completion as per the CA and completion for the purpose of tolling, the IE rightly clarified both and stated that these two cannot be linked.

9. RE-ISSUE OF PCOD POST ELIMINATION OF DISCONTINUITIES

9.1) The Concessionaire repeatedly protested against the Authority's unjust action of non-endorsement of PCOD issued by the IE on the grounds of discontinuity, which was against the provisions of the CA. While the Concessionaire patiently awaited payment of Annuity together with payment of delay days as per Article 28.1 of the CA, in the meantime, using its own financing, went on completing more and more additional areas as and when the vacant access and Right of Way to such areas were made available to the Concessionaire, which too was in small beats and pieces, even after several months past the cut-off limit of Appointed Date plus 90 days.

9.2) A high-level meeting was convened on ... during which it was assured that PCOD will be cleared by ... Subsequently, another review meeting was held on ... During this meeting also, it was agreed that PCOD for the Project will be considered by ... The Concessionaire vide letter dated ... **(Ref. 54)** reminded IE with a request for the issuance of COD along with the determination of the delay days.

9.3) Subsequent to the removal of hindrances by the Authority in some of the discontinuities, the concessionaire eliminated those discontinuities and again conducted COD tests on ... and the results were submitted to the IE vide letter dated ... **(Ref. 55).** The results of COD tests, which were conducted earlier in ... were also resubmitted. Despite a slowdown/stoppage of funding by Lenders and a huge increase in interest payments on debt during the construction, and a substantial increase in capital costs on account of inflation and an increase in other costs, the Concessionaire again completed the available hindrance-free area.

9.4) The IE again declared Project Highway fit for commercial operations and sought formal consent from the Authority for the issue of a **Provisional Certificate of Completion on ... (Ref. 56).** The IE confirmed that the Concessionaire has eliminated discontinuities that were vacated by the Authority. The IE reiterated that, in terms of Article 10.3.5 of the CA, PCOD can't be delayed on account of Vacant access not being granted to the Concessionaire.

9.5) Though the Lenders were unwilling to provide any further finance in view of the abnormal delay in the commencement of Annuity payments, the Concessionaire kept on pursuing the Lenders and after considerable perusal, they agreed to provide an additional fund amounting to Rs.

100 crores for expeditious completion of the balance Works provided a provisional COD was issued by the Authority. This decision of Lenders was communicated to the Employer vide letter dated … **(Ref. 57).**

9.6) The Authority constituted a high-level committee comprising of three CGMs and the said Committee inspected the entire Project Highway on … and witnessed each and every hindrance existing on that date.

9.7) A high-level meeting was convened on … when the lender was also present. During the meeting, the lender was directed to provide further finance as the Annuity had not commenced to date because of hindrances, and the Concessionaire was assured that the Employer would issue PCOD and commence payment of the Annuity upon making four-laning continuous and that the decision on slipped Annuities and delay days would also be taken based on recommendation of the IE. The Concessionaire went on to explain that even after over 1688 days past the Appointed Date hindrances exist at various locations, and as per Article 10.3.5 areas affected by hindrances even as on Appointed Date plus 90 days cannot come in the way of PCOD and hence holding back PCOD for hindrances not removed even after 1688 days of Appointed Date is highly unjust. MOM of the above meeting, dated … is enclosed herewith **(Ref. 58).**

9.8) Even after the high-level meeting, the pace of the removal of hindrances did not pick up. The Concessionaire regularly kept on reminding for the removal of hindrances, stating that the same cannot continue for an indefinitely prolonged period. In this regard, the Concessionaire's letter dated … **(Ref. 59)** is self-explanatory, wherein twenty photographs capturing the hindrances were enclosed. Even from the data furnished in **Annexure 4**, you will observe that in a period of … months past the above high-level meeting, an incremental ROW of only … Hec. could be acquired despite the best efforts by the Employer, which clearly shows the insurmountableness and severity of hindrances.

9.9) The Employer has been personally following up with DMs of both Districts for the removal of hindrances. In this regard, attention is drawn to the Authority's letter dated … to DM. **(Ref. 60)** which comprehensively lists all hindrances in that District and seeks the support of the Administration in vacating these hindrances.

9.10) However, even after a lapse of 2148 days beyond Appointed Date, when land acquisition issues in a thickly populated, busy, and highly encumbered Market area from ... km to ... km and two other discontinuities remained unresolved, and when it was realised that providing land for four-laning of a continuous stretch of even 41 km is not possible, a high-level meeting was convened on ... discontinuity at the market area and other two locations were allowed for the purpose of COD. The MOM of the above meeting was circulated vide Letter dated ... **(Ref. 60).**

9.11) Based on the above MOM, eventually, the PCOD was issued by the IE on 1-09-2016 (i.e. on 2213rd day from Appointed Date) vide letter dated ... **(Ref. 61)** after obtaining fresh consent from the Employer and this consent was given only and this consent was given only when Project Highway became toll-worthy, toll notification was published in newspapers, a toll-collecting agency was appointed through e-tendering and the toll could be started.

10. EFFECT OF FORCE MAJEURE EVENTS ON CONCESSION

In addition to delay on account of not providing vacant access and Right of Way, and non-procurement of (effective) approval of the Railway Authorities, the performance of the Concessionaire and his obligations under the CA were also affected by a few Force Majeure Events that had impeded the implementation of the Project even on Site acquired and provided by the Authority. The effect of such Force Majeure Events on Concession needs to be determined. We have been notifying these Force Majeure events to the Authority and the IE from time to time through various communication, discussions, and meetings apart from escalating this to the highest levels, and are well documented on record. Among various such delays, a few major events are briefly presented in a consolidated manner herein below, together with their effect on Concession:

10.1 Political Events

Following are the acts/events that were caused by Government instrumentality:

a) Government Order restricting vehicle movements on the bridge

The ... bridge is the most important link for approaching the Site location from the southern part of the State. Aggregates were procured from crusher plants from the southern area, and we had also installed our crusher in this area. Aggregates were brought from this area using ten-wheeled trucks. However, when the condition of the bridge started deteriorating, the Government imposed restrictions on the movement of ten-wheeled vehicles from year ... and eventually the movement of ten-wheeled vehicles on this bridge was completely prohibited with effect from ..., which was formally reiterated vide Government Order dated ... **(Ref. 62)**. As a result, supply of aggregates from the southern part was compulsorily stopped, and we had to depend on local suppliers who neither could supply aggregate of good quality meeting technical specifications nor could supply the required quantity to meet our schedule.

The effect of the above Force Majeure Event on Concession has been ... days as worked out in **Annexure 7.1**.

b) Government Order banning sand mining

State Government issued an order dated ... **(Ref. 63)** banning all mining activities in the State as per the order by National Green Tribunal, Eastern Zone, dated ...

As a result of the above ban, the supply of sand was completely stopped.

This Force Majeure event was notified vide letter dated ... **(Ref. 64)**.

During this period, we tried to shift sand from our internal stockyard, but shifting sand even from our internal stockyard was also not allowed and was prohibited as per the letter dated ... from the Mining Department **(Ref. 65)**.

The effect of the above Force Majeure Event on Concession has been ... days as worked out in **Annexure 7.2**.

c) District Magistrate's Order restricting the movement of vehicles due to Kawarias:

Every year in the month of Shravan of the Hindu Calendar (i.e. July / August), thousands of Kawaria go walking barefooted up to ... temple through Project Highway. Because of this annual religious activity, there are several restrictions on the movement of construction vehicles and even passenger vehicles.

The large movement of Kawarias continues for the whole month of Shravan, but from Thursday/Friday to Monday, the flow of Kawarias increases substantially, and Kawariya in large nos. walk along the Project Highway stretch to perform 'Jala Abhishek' on auspicious Mondays of the month of Shravan.

There were no restrictions during the year. but when a couple of fatal accidents involving Kawarias occurred in year ..., Kawarias started agitation, resulting in serious law and order issues. Since then, as a precautionary measure, DM has been ordering complete stoppage of all vehicles between Friday to Monday on weeks 1, 4 & 5, and between Thursday to Monday for weeks 2 & 3 for the month of Shravan every year. Thus, for a period of one month every year and between every Thursday/Friday afternoon to Monday afternoon, the movement of not only construction vehicles but even passenger vehicles is completely stopped, bringing all work to stand still during this period.

One typical order from DM on traffic restrictions dated ... for the year ... is enclosed **(Ref. 66)** which is self-explanatory.

The effect of the above Force Majeure Event on Concession has been ... days as worked out in **Annexure 7.3**.

10.2 Indirect Political Events

The Concessionaire's camp was subjected to attacks by mobs on two occasions, setting on fire various equipment like JCB, Grader Roller,

Dumpers, etc. These law and order violation events were notified to the Employer under Articles 34.5.1 & 34.5.2 of the CA vide letter dated … **(Ref. 67),** and dated … **(Ref. 68)**.

The Employer took up the matter with the State Authorities and the State Government wrote to the Director General, Police to take the matter seriously and ensure adequate security **(Ref. 69)**.

The effects of the above two Force Majeure Events on Concession have been … days and … days, as worked out in **Annexures 7.4.** and **7.5**.

10.3 Non-Political Events

a) Unprecedented heavy rains and floods in …

Unprecedented heavy rain at the project site on … severely affected camps at … Km, at … Km and all working stretches of Highway and structures from Km … to Km … and entire bypass. The downpour was so intense and unprecedented that flood waters completely inundated the entire project site.

This Force Majeure event was notified vide letter dated **(Ref. 70)**.

The effect of the above Force Majeure Event on Concession has been … days as worked out in **Annexure 7.6**.

b) Unprecedented Cyclone …

The State was under the influence of an unprecedented cyclone on … and … The accompanying heavy rains submerged almost all of the working locations, including the area near Concessionaire's camps.

This Force Majeure event was notified vide letter dated … **(Ref. 71)**.

IE confirmed vide letter dated … **(Ref. 72)** that the aggregate stockyard, Hot mix plant, concrete batching plant and WMM plant were still flooded in … Camp though concrete batching plant at … camp has been made operational since …, and the concreting works are likely to be resumed in a few days.

The effect of the above Force Majeure Event on Concession has been ... days as worked out in **Annexure 7.7.**

Since the above Force Majeure Events have occurred after the Appointed Date and before COD, the Concession Period and the dates set forth in the Project Completion Schedule need to be extended as per Article 34.6.2 of the CA.

11. IMPACT OF CHANGE OF SCOPE WORKS ON PROJECT COMPLETION SCHEDULE

During the execution of the Project, many changes were found necessary vis-a-vis what was stipulated in the CA. Also, there were local issues and demands for VUP, PUP etc. The IE and the Employer examined all such issues and ordered the Change of Scope Works. Since the above Change of Scope Works ordered by the Authority were required to be carried out during the Construction Period, the impact of these Change of Scope Works had on the Project Completion Schedule are required to be determined as per Article 16.2.2 of the CA.

TABLE 3 below shows the Change of Scope Works together with its impact on Project Completion Schedule:

The impact of the above COS Works on the Project Completion Schedule has been ... days as worked out in **Annexure 8.1** and **Annexure 8.2**.

12. EXTENSION OF PROJECT MILESTONES

12.1) Schedule G of the CA, stipulates that the Concessionaire shall comply with the requirements set therein for each of the Project Milestones and Scheduled Four-Laning Date.

12.2) As explained in para 3 and 4 above, there have been substantial delays in Land Acquisition. The Concessionaire through its own liaisoning effort, could work in some of the areas where land compensation was not paid. Though these liaisoning efforts could not help in achieving progress as per the accelerated programme planned by the Concessionaire, these efforts, coupled with the mobilisation of ample resources by the Concessionaire helped in achieving better progress than specified in Schedule G of the CA in the initial stages i.e. in Project Milestone –I and II as can be seen from the enclosed **Annexure 9** titled 'Project Completion Schedule: Requirements As Per Schedule- G v/s Actual Achievements'. Of course, after Project Milestone II when the delays in Land Acquisition persisted even more predominantly and the pace of acquiring land continued to remain very slow, this material default not only prevented the Concessionaire from achieving COD prior to the Scheduled Four-Laning Date but also caused a delay in achieving subsequent Project Milestones viz. Project Milestone III and Scheduled Four-Laning Date and thus resulted in the delay in achieving COD. Thus, in view of the Material Defaults in providing vacant access and Right of Way and other causes, the Project Milestones and Scheduled Four-Laning Date stipulated in Schedule G have been rendered inapplicable.

12.3) The Concessionaire submitted a request for revision of Milestones vide letter dated … **(Ref. 73).** The Concessionaire contended that the Schedule of Completion in the CA is contemplated based on the fulfilment of obligations by the Authority pertaining to providing vacant access to land required and necessary for four-laning on Appointed Date and Appointed Date plus 90 days. However, even in …, i.e. nearly six months after the SPCD, land was yet to be provided, thereby rendering the Milestones stipulated in the CA inapplicable. The Concessionaire also stated that even for Project Milestones III, progress actually achieved exceeded percentage progress required as per Schedule G when compared with the percentage of the site actually made available as on the Appointed Date plus 90 days and subsequently.

12.4) Taking cognisance of the Concessionaire's aforementioned request, the IE recommended, vide letter dated … **(Ref. 74)**, that the Authority may kindly consider Extension of Project Milestones and the Scheduled Four-Laning Date in accordance with para 6 of Schedule G of the CA.

12.5) Subsequently, the IE made another recommendation vide letter ref dated … **(Ref. 75)** stating that the earlier recommendation made on … for extension of Construction Period up to … was based on the assumption that balance land will be made available by … and since the status of balance unencumbered land has not very much changed between … and

…, the IE recommended provisional extension of Construction Period by 857 days, i.e. up to …, subject to the condition that balance land is provided by … The IE also stated in the said letter that the issue of delay days under Article 28.1 will be examined after the completion of the Project.

12.6) Reference is kindly invited to Para 6 of Schedule G which stipulates that upon extension of any or all of the Project Milestones or Scheduled Four-Laning Date under and in accordance with the provisions of the CA, the Project Completion Schedule shall be deemed to have been amended accordingly.

12.7) Though the delays that have taken place are substantially more, the Concessionaire requests IE to extend Project Milestone I, II and III and Scheduled Four-Laning Date under and in accordance with the provisions of CA as per Table 4 below, which allows a period of … months from the date of PCOD i.e. … for the completion of balance works provided vacant access and Right of Way for balance areas is made available within 90 days from the date of PCOD:

13. From the events and facts described in the foregoing, the following issues emerge:

13.1) It is the Authority's fundamental obligation to provide to the Concessionaire the Vacant access and Right of Way to the Site in accordance with the provisions of Article 10.3.1 and satisfying the requirements of Article 10.3.2 on or prior to the Appointed Date. Also, in accordance with Article 10.4 of the CA, the site shall be made available free from all Encumbrances and occupations.

13.2) On Appointed Date, vacant access and Right of Way to only … Hect. land was provided out of … Hect. land required and necessary for four-laning which in terms of length is only … Km on LHS and… Km on RHS.

13.3) The Concessionaire on his part, diligently took up field survey work, geotechnical soil investigation work, preparation of designs and drawings, etc. immediately upon signing the CA, and also started site mobilisation in the right earnest for undertaking expeditious and fast-track implementation of the Project. The Concessionaire established three Camps and also invested huge amounts of money in procuring Plant and

Equipment and mobilised three independent sets of fleets of Plant and Equipment for accelerated implementation of the Project. The mobilisation done by the Concessionaire clearly establishes sincere intention on the part of the Concessionaire to complete Four-Laning much ahead of the Scheduled Four-Laning Date and to achieve COD prior to the Scheduled Four-Laning Date.

13.4) On the Appointed Date plus 90 days, vacant access and Right of Way to only … Hect of land (which in terms of length is only … km on LHS and … km on RHS) was provided to the Concessionaire and that too was in several discontinuous stretches.

13.5) The pace of acquiring ROW has been quite slow, and the delays persisted for a substantially prolonged period beyond the cut-off date of the Appointed Date plus 90 days. Thus, the fundamental obligation necessary for performance by the Concessionaire has not been fulfilled by the Authority and there has been a Material Default on this count. This default had a Material Adverse Effect on the Concessionaire causing a material financial burden, and accordingly, the Concessionaire is entitled to all reliefs and compensations as per the provisions of the CA.

13.6) Because of the mobilisation of three sets of Plant and Equipment and its own liaisoning effort of personal negotiations with Landowners, the Concessionaire achieved Project Milestones I and II more than 60 days ahead and also could make Four-lane traffic through in many of the stretches from … ahead of Project Completion Schedule at Schedule G albeit with discontinuities that were caused by hindrances.

13.7) Acknowledging the fact that even after a lapse of … months past the expiry of the Construction Period, the Project was subjected to insurmountable hindrances at multiple locations; the Employer gave a directive to delink the above hindrance affected portion and to put the rest of the stretch to Commercial Operations and gave consent to issue a Provisional COD on the above basis. Accordingly, the IE declared Project Highway fit for entering into Commercial Operations on … under Article 10.3.5 of the CA and sought formal post-issuance approval from the Employer. On the date of PCOD Four-lane traffic facility was available for as much as ... km out of ... km stretch excluding Bypass i.e., albeit with a few discontinuities that were caused by hindrances.

13.8) Article 10.3.5 explicitly states that the issue of a Provisional Certificate shall not be affected or delayed on account of vacant access to any part of the Site not being granted to the Concessionaire or any construction on such part of the Site remaining incomplete on the date of Tests on account of delay or denial of such access thereto. Accordingly, the Concessionaire is entitled to COD as issued by the IE together with the delay days that occurred until then. However, Annuity payments were not commenced by the Authority and surprisingly, in gross violation of the provisions of the CA, the Authority decided to make further attempts to eliminate discontinuities in land acquisition at this belated stage of the Project completely ignoring the cut-off date of Appointed Date plus 90 days and thereby went on compounding Authority Event of Default more and more.

13.9) The magnitude and severity of the difficulties faced by the District Administration and the Authority in obtaining Vacant Access can be appreciated by the fact that in order to provide vacant access and Right of Way to the Concessionaire, the District Administration and the Employer had to conduct several demolition drives accompanied by the armed Police force amidst stiff local resistance as shown in TABLE 1 which continued in ... and ..., i.e. as late as 2180 days past Appointed date as shown in Table 5 below and notified through **Ref. 76** to **Ref. 79**:

The demolition drive conducted between ... to ... under the leadership of ... has been the biggest demolition drive so far in the State and has been quite successful.

13.10) Eventually, the PCOD was issued by the IE only on ... (i.e. on the 2213rd day from the Appointed Date) after obtaining fresh prior consent from the Employer and this consent was given only when Project Highway became toll-worthy, toll notification was published in newspapers, a toll-collecting agency was appointed through e-tendering and the toll could be started. It is extremely painful to point out that the Employer linked the issue of PCOD with the completion of the project from toll worthiness point of view, in gross violation of the fundamental provisions of the CA on which the Concession was based.

13.11) The above inordinate delay in commencing the Annuity resulted in a slowdown/stoppage of funding by the Lenders and a huge increase in interest payments on debt, a substantial increase in capital costs on account of inflation, and an increase in other costs.

13.12) Thus, the Authority has not only materially defaulted in complying with provisions of the CA as regards its fundamental obligation of providing vacant access to the Site to the Concessionaire as stipulated in the CA, but also the Authority went on compounding the default more and more by not commencing Annuity Payments and these defaults had a cascading Material Adverse Effect on the Concessionaire causing a material financial burden.

14. Cause and Effect Analysis

As stated above, the causes that resulted in delays in achieving COD include delays in providing vacant access and Right of Way to the site on the Appointed Date and even thereafter for a substantially prolonged period, Force Majeure Events, introduction of COS items ordered by the Authority that were required to be carried out during the Construction Period. These causes of delay and disruptions had cascading effects on the concession, which are briefly summarised and presented in enclosed **Annexure 10** together with references to the relevant provisions in the CA.

15. Even as on …, the vacant access and Right of Way in … Km in LHS and … Km in RHS is not available to the Concessionaire for the execution of the Works as detailed in enclosed **Annexure 11.1 to 11.4**:

You will observe from the above Annexures that many cases are sub judice either in DLAO or in Arbitration or in the High Court, and we are not sure when these matters will reach finality through the legal process.

16. In view of the foregoing, the Concessionaire submits that the number of days by which COD has preceded the Scheduled Four-Laning Date, including an aggregate number of delay days caused by Political Force Majeure Event and Authority Event of Default needs to be determined and certified by IE.

Since vacant access and Right of Way to a few locations are still not provided and new Change of Scope items are being ordered, application of a further number of days of delay, if any, beyond ... will be submitted in due course.

The Concessionaire requests the IE to examine our above submissions and requests the IE to kindly:

a) extend the Concession Period and the dates set forth in the Project Completion Schedule arising because of the occurrence of Force Majeure Events as per Article 34.6.2 of the CA as submitted by the Concessionaire in para 10 above;

b) determine the impact of Change of Scope items ordered by the Authority on the Project Completion Schedule as per Article 16.2.2 of the CA as submitted by the Concessionaire in para 11 above;

c) extend Project Milestones I, II and III and Scheduled Four-Laning Date under and in accordance with the provisions of the CA as submitted in Table 4 of para 12 above.

d) determine and certify the number of days by which COD has preceded the Scheduled Four-Laning Date, including an aggregate number of days of delay caused by Political Force Majeure Event and Authority Event of Default as per Article 28.1 of the CA as submitted by the Concessionaire in para 5 to 11

In case you need any further clarification or supporting documents, we shall be pleased to furnish the same upon hearing from your good self.

Thanking you, and assuring you of our best attention always,

Encl:

Appendices

VOLUME	ANNEXURE	TITLE		Page No.
VOL. I	Annexure 1	List of Major Plants and Equipment mobilised by the Concessionaire		
	Annexure 2	Land acquisition status as on Appointed Date.		
	Annexure 3	Land acquisition status as on Appointed Date plus 90 days.		
	Annexure 4	Land acquisition status on Appointed Date, Appointed Date plus 90 days and month-wise for subsequent periods.		
	Annexure 5	Land acquisition status as on SPCD		
	Annexure 6	Strip Chart for Bypass		
	Annexure 7	7.1	Force Majeure Event: Government Order restricting vehicle movements on the bridge	
		7.2	Force Majeure Event: Government Order banning sand mining	
		7.3	Force Majeure Event: District Magistrate's Order restricting the movement of Vehicles due to Kawarias	
		7.4	Force Majeure Event: Attack at … camp	
		7.5	Force Majeure Event: Attack at … camp	
		7.6	Force Majeure Event: Unprecedented heavy rains and floods in …	
		7.7	Force Majeure Event: Cyclone in the State on …	

Annexure 8	8.1	COS: Underpass at …
	8.2	COS: Additional Box Culverts
Annexure 9	Project Completion Schedule: Requirements As Per Schedule- G v/s Actual Achievements	
Annexure 10	Cause and Effect Analysis	
Annexure 11	11.1	Non-availability of vacant access in Non-PCOD stretch: Ch. … km to … km
	11.2	Non-availability of vacant access in PCOD stretch: Ch. … km to … km
	11.3	Non-availability of vacant access in Non-PCOD stretch: Ch. … km to … km
	11.4	Non-availability of vacant access in Non-PCOD stretch: Bypass … km to … km
VOL. II	Containing **Ref 1 to 40** for ready reference	
VOL. III	Containing **Ref 41 to 79** for ready reference	

APPENDIX 7

DO LETTERS

Demi-official letters, popularly known as DO letters, are in quite common use, especially in Government departments. It is used as one of the most important means of correspondence between Government officers to draw the personal attention of the addressee. In many situations, it is more prudent to use personal relationships rather than official channels of communication. DO letters help in resolving issues through personal relationships.

Following is a typical example of a DO letter from a Government officer of one Government department to his counterpart in another Government department which shows how personal relationships can help in the expeditious resolution of issues:

> Dear Mr. ...,
>
> Mr. ..., the Project Director from our Project Office at ... has submitted GA drawing for the proposed Rail-Over-Bridge at ... a couple of months back.
>
> Other works in this stretch are going on in full swing. We need to start ROB work on priority.
>
> I solicit your personal intervention in expediting GA drawing approval from your department at the earliest. This will help us synchronise ROB completion with the completion of other works on this stretch.
>
> I will meet you sometime next week at your kind convenience so that I can personally explain the urgency of the matter.
>
> Sincerely,

APPENDIX 8

BUSSINESS LETTER: A TYPICAL FORMAT

	ABC Limited XYZ Street MUMBAI ---
Date ➡	Date: April 25, 2024
Name, designation, and address ➡	Mr. A. B. Gowda, Chief Product Manager, M/s PQR Software Limited, Bengaluru …
Salutation ➡	Dear Sir,
Subject ➡	Sub: Inconsistent outputs from the software
Reference ➡	Ref: Our Purchase Order No. … Dated …
Opening para ➡	As you are aware, we purchased state-of-the-art software from you last month. The software was installed by your team, and initialisation was also carried out by them.

Middle para →	We've been using this software since three weeks. However, it appears that there are programming bugs in the software. When we compared software outputs with manual results, we discovered inconsistencies in the results. Yours being a reputed company, we thought we would have a perfect solution for our business needs. However, we are rather surprised to see these inconsistencies in your software.
Concluding para →	We request that you depute your representative immediately and resolve the above issues.
Complimentary close →	Thanking you,
Signature →	Sd/
Name →	(C.D. Trivedi)
Designation →	Chief Information Officer ABC Limited

12

BIBLIOGRAPHY

1. Brayan A. Garner
   'HBR Guide to Better Business Writing'
2. Bill Birchard
   'The Science of Strong Business Writing'
3. Flesch, Rudolf
   'The Art of Plain Talk'
4. Kenneth Roman and Joel Raphaelson
   'Writing that Works'
5. Laura Brown and Rich Karlgaard
   'The Only Business Writing Book You'll Ever Need'

ABOUT THE AUTHOR

$\mathcal{M}$. U. Shah, a Civil Engineering graduate, has a scholarly, distinguished academic career and an illustrious professional journey. He has worked on various prestigious infrastructure projects in India and North Africa and has been accredited with several exemplary achievements.

A distinguished alumnus of the National Institute of Construction Management and Research, he is the recipient of a Lifetime Achievement Award.

An inspiring speaker, a trainer, and a passionate writer, he has authored several papers on technical and managerial topics. He has represented various Technical Committee of The Bureau of Indian Standards and the Indian Roads Congress. He has chaired and co-chaired several technical sessions and served as a panelist at various seminars and conferences. He has been the Editor of Gammon Bulletin for over twenty-five years.

He is a distinguished faculty member for various training programme in India and abroad. His flagship workshops on the topic of Excellence are immensely popular. So far, over 2500 participants have attended these workshops.

OTHER PUBLICATIONS BY THE AUTHOR

www.ingramcontent.com/pod-product-compliance
Lightning Source LLC
LaVergne TN
LVHW041706070526
838199LV00045B/1221